D1058929

AMERICAN STORIES

*Washington's Cherry Tree, Lincoln's Log Cabin
and Other Tales— True and Not-So-True—
and How They Spread Throughout the Land*

PAUL ARON

Guilford, Connecticut

An imprint of The Rowman & Littlefield Publishing Group, Inc.
4501 Forbes Blvd., Ste. 200
Lanham, MD 20706
www.rowman.com

Distributed by NATIONAL BOOK NETWORK

Copyright © 2020 Paul Aron

All rights reserved. No part of this book may be reproduced in any form or by any electronic or mechanical means, including information storage and retrieval systems, without written permission from the publisher, except by a reviewer who may quote passages in a review.

British Library Cataloguing in Publication Information available

Library of Congress Cataloging-in-Publication Data available

ISBN 978-1-4930-4232-6 (cloth alk. paper)
ISBN 978-1-4930-4233-3 (electronic)

♾™ The paper used in this publication meets the minimum requirements of American National Standard for Information Sciences—Permanence of Paper for Printed Library Materials, ANSI/NISO Z39.48-1992.

CONTENTS

PREFACE

DEBUNKING—THE WORD, NOT THE CONCEPT—WAS INVENTED BY W. E. Woodward in his 1923 novel, *Bunk*. Woodward was himself a master debunker, as evidenced in his 1926 biography of George Washington.

"The Cannot-Tell-a-Lie incident of the cherry tree and the hatchet is a brazen piece of fiction," Woodward wrote, "made up by a minister named the Rev. Mason L. Weems, who wrote a life of our country's father which is stuffed with this and similar fables."

Most of Woodward's readers probably already suspected that young George never actually took a hatchet to his father's favorite tree and then redeemed himself by confessing. Biographers and historians had skewered Parson Weems long before Woodward got to it. In 1800—the same year Weems's biography was published—the *Monthly Magazine and American Review* called the book "as entertaining and edifying matter as can be found in the annals of fanaticism and absurdity." Since then, there have been plenty of books written to separate the myths of American history from the reality.

Do we need another? Well, in a world where fake history can spread as fast as fake news, there's always room for a good debunking. But this book has a different focus. Rather than simply exposing myths for what they are, it traces them to their origins and then follows their evolution. In the process, I hope, this book suggests why these myths spread far and wide.

The story of the cherry tree, for example, tells us nothing about George Washington's actual childhood, but surely it tells us something about what Americans wanted in the father of their country—an incorruptible man. Along the same lines, the story of Betsy Ross's flag tells us nothing about how the Stars and Stripes came to be but tells us something about what Americans, or at least some Americans, wanted in a founding mother. The Ross story was first told in 1870, one year after Elizabeth Cady Stanton and Susan B. Anthony founded the National Woman Suffrage Association. Amidst this challenge to traditional gender roles, many undoubtedly found it reassuring to find a heroine who stayed home to sew.

The stories told about American history—both true and false—have themselves changed the course of history. Davy Crockett may not have died at the Alamo, but stories of his heroic stand inspired other Americans to defeat Mexican forces in Texas. Abraham Lincoln may not have been born in the log cabin that millions of Americans have visited in Kentucky, but that cabin inspired many to believe that they, too, could rise from humble origins to become whatever they wanted, even president of the United States. The antebellum South may not have been populated by chivalric gentlemen and glamorous belles and happy servants, but this romantic view of the past helped reconcile North and South after the Civil War—and also helped reestablish whites' control of southern politics.

Sometimes these stories led people to act for the good, sometimes not, but they most definitely mattered. "For very, very much history," said historian William Dunning, "there is more importance in the ancient error than in the new-found truth." Dunning spoke those words in 1913, but they remain true today.

CHAPTER ONE

The Flat Earth

WHEN CHRISTOPHER COLUMBUS PROPOSED TO THE KING AND QUEEN of Spain that he could reach lands to the east by sailing west, the monarchs sought the advice of experts. A council was convened at the University of Salamanca in 1486 and its members raised a number of objections to Columbus's plan. According to Columbus's son Ferdinand, who joined his father on his fourth voyage to the New World and later wrote his biography, some of the learned geographers argued that the world was so large that to reach Asia would take years. Others thought that the ocean was unnavigable. Still others believed that "because the world was round" it would be impossible to return to Spain; the trip west would be downhill but the return trip "would be like sailing a ship to the top of a mountain."

The council recommended Ferdinand and Isabella not finance Columbus's voyage and, for the moment, Columbus was stymied.

But note the council's reasons. Contrary to the oft-told tale, they most decidedly did not rebuff Columbus because they believed the earth was flat. On the contrary: They calculated, correctly, that the globe was too large for Columbus to reach China or Japan via a westward route. Had there been no land between Europe and Asia, Columbus and his crew would likely have perished.

Of course, there were some people in the fifteenth century who believed that the world was flat and that anyone sailing west across the ocean would fall off its edge. Some people in the twenty-first century believe that. But most educated people, including most on the council at Salamanca, knew better.

How, then, did the flat-earth myth spread far and wide?

This was largely the work of Washington Irving, best known for his fictional creations like Rip Van Winkle, who falls asleep and wakes up twenty years later. It was Irving who planted in the American imagination an image of the enlightened discoverer thwarted by medieval ignorance. Irving's 1828 biography of Columbus presented a hero in many ways as fictional as Rip Van Winkle.

The context of the Salamanca conference, Irving made clear, was the Inquisition. "The era was distinguished . . . for the prevalence of religious zeal, and Spain surpassed all other countries of Christendom in the fervor of her devotion," wrote Irving. "Every opinion that savored of heresy made its owner obnoxious to odium and persecution." And so Columbus "was assailed with citations from the bible and the testament" as well as "the expositions of various saints and reverend commentators."

Continued Irving: "To his simplest proposition, the spherical form of the earth, were opposed figurative texts of scripture. They observed that in the Psalms the heavens are said to be extended like . . . the curtain or covering of a tent . . . and that St. Paul . . . compares the heavens to a . . . tent, extended over the earth, which they thence inferred must be flat." They quoted Lactantius, a third-century Christian writer who asked whether "there are any so foolish . . . as to believe that . . . there is a part of the world in which all things are topsy-turvy: where the trees grow with their branches downward, and where it rains, hails and snows upward?"

Columbus tried to explain his reasoning; "but there was a preponderating mass of inert bigotry, and learned pride . . . which refused to yield." It took another six years for Columbus to convince Ferdinand and Isabella to take a chance on his voyage.

There is much irony to the myth of Columbus facing off against religious extremists, since in reality Columbus was himself a devout Christian. It is also ironic that Columbus is presented as the champion of a round earth, since later in his life he came to believe that the earth was *not* round.

Columbus reached that conclusion during his third voyage to what by then he suspected was not an island off the coast of China or Japan but a new world. In 1498, Columbus wrote a letter to Ferdinand and Isabella describing his latest discovery.

"I have come to another conclusion respecting the earth," Columbus wrote, "namely, that it is not round . . . but of the form of a pear, which is very round except where the stalk grows, at which part it is most prominent; or like a round ball, upon one part of which is a prominence like a woman's nipple."

On this third of his voyages, Columbus believed he had not only found a new continent but that it was the site of the Garden of Eden. "I am convinced that it is the spot of the earthly paradise," his letter to Ferdinand and Isabella continued, "whither no one can go but by God's permission."

Ferdinand and Isabella must have read the letter with dismay. The letter was a strange mix of geography and religion—and entirely delusional. Historians have debated whether the letter represented the decline of Columbus's once-brilliant mind into madness, or whether his voyages were from the start motivated by a religious fervor. Either way, by the time Ferdinand and Isabella received the letter, they had already grown disillusioned with Columbus. Despite his genius as an explorer, he was an incompetent administrator; the lands he governed in Spain's name were in a state of chaos, with both the native people and the Spanish colonists in rebellion. The king and queen sent a new conquistador to take over, and Columbus was returned to Spain in chains.

Columbus eventually managed to work his way back into the good graces of the king and queen, at least enough so that they gave their support to a fourth voyage—or maybe the monarchs felt that sending him on another trip was the easiest way to be rid of his complaints. Still, as far as history was concerned, Columbus remained largely out of favor over the next couple of centuries. The Spanish preferred to hear of the exploits of conquistadors like Cortés and Pizarro, who conquered the great Inca and Aztec empires. The British, who planted their first lasting colony at

Jamestown in 1607 but who even before then had begun to develop an empire to rival Spain's, condemned Columbus and the Spanish in general for their brutal treatment of native peoples. (The British view was valid but hypocritical, given how they would eventually treat the Indians of North America.)

Columbus's disrepute opened the door for Amerigo Vespucci, the explorer famous for having two continents named after him without actually discovering either. Vespucci was not entirely undeserving of the honor; unlike Columbus, who despite his claim to have discovered paradise might still have thought he was near Asia, Vespucci was certain he had discovered a "New World" and he called it just that. Besides, it was not Vespucci himself but the German mapmaker Martin Waldseemüller who in 1507 suggested the new land be called America. Nonetheless, devotees of Columbus, who felt America ought to be called Columbia, would brand Vespucci an undeserving usurper.

Those devotees grew more numerous and more prominent in the eighteenth century, as Americans began to see themselves as a people separate from Europeans and eager to push into a new frontier. What better hero could there have been than Columbus, who also left Europe to head west? The trend became even more pronounced with the Revolution. At first, some patriots preferred to call America Columba or Columbina, but Columbia emerged as the clear favorite and, in the form of a woman, the personification of the new nation. The patriot poet Mercy Otis Warren wrote in 1775 of "Columbia's distant fertile Plains" where "Liberty a happy Goddess reigns." Joel Barlow's "Vision of Columbus" was published in 1787 and was paid for in part by subscribers who included George Washington (who bought twenty copies) and Benjamin Franklin (who bought six). Barlow later revised and retitled his poem; the 1807 version was titled "The Columbiad" and ran an epic 7,350 lines.

America never changed its name to Columbia, of course. But in 1784 King's College in New York became Columbia College. In 1787 Timothy Dwight wrote the popular song "Columbia." In 1791, the federal district that was to become the nation's capital was named the Territory of Columbia. And about fifty towns and cities in the United States eventually took the explorer's name.

Books for children sang the praises of Columbus's ingenuity. The 1811 *Columbian Reader* told how Columbus, back in Spain, was faced with accusations that his discovery was nothing but luck. He called for an egg and asked if any of those belittling him could make it stand on its little end. Everyone said it was impossible.

Then,

Columbus, striking it gently, flattened the shell till it stood upright on the table. The company with a disdainful sneer, cried out, "anybody might have done it." "Yes (said Columbus), but none of you thought of it; so I discovered the Indies, and now every pilot can steer the same course. Many things appear easy when once performed, though before they were thought impossible."

The story of the flattened egg had been told before about Columbus and, for that matter, about others whose pioneering work was later denigrated. No matter. For nineteenth-century Americans, the story captured how they liked to think of Columbus—and themselves.

More than anyone else, the writer who made Columbus an American hero was Washington Irving. Irving's original plan was to translate from Spanish to English a spate of newly surfaced documents pertaining to Columbus. But the novelist in Irving could not resist embellishing the historical record, and the biography he ended up writing interpreted the documents, new and old, in a manner that could be described as elastic.

Take, for example, the story of the mutiny of Columbus's crew. In his biography of his father, Ferdinand Columbus reported the "grumbling, lamenting, and plotting" of the crew as they grew increasingly fearful they would never find land. Irving expanded on "the constant danger there was of open and desperate rebellion" against Columbus, which included plans to "throw him into the sea, and give out on their arrival in Spain, that he had fallen overboard." Through all this, Irving added, Columbus "kept a serene and steady countenance."

Or there's the story of how Columbus's voyage was financed. The royal treasury was depleted by war with the Moors, and Ferdinand Columbus reported that Isabella had offered her jewels to help pay for the expedition. Irving's version was more dramatic.

"The generous spirit of Isabella was enkindled," Irving wrote. "How could she draw on an exhausted treasury for a measure to which the king was adverse! . . . With an enthusiasm worthy of herself, and of the cause, Isabella exclaimed, 'I undertake the enterprise for my own crown of Castile, and will pledge my private jewels to raise the necessary funds.'" The Cuban novelist Alejo Carpentier extended Isabella's enthusiasm from the cause to the bedroom; in his 1978 novel *The Harp and the Shadow,* Isabella's promise to provide Columbus the ships he needs comes during the "nights of our intimacy."

But back to Irving: His Columbus was "a man of great and inventive genius." His discoveries "enlightened the ignorance of that age . . . and dispelled numerous errors with which he himself had been obliged to struggle." His failures were largely those of "the dissolute rabble which it was his misfortune to command." As for his transporting the Indians to Spain to sell as slaves? Irving did not entirely exonerate Columbus, but this was the "bigotry of the age." Besides, Columbus "was goaded on by the mercenary impatience of the crown."

Numerous others followed in Irving's wake.

In 1836 Congress commissioned the neoclassicist John Vanderlyn to paint the *Landing of Columbus.* It was installed in the Capitol Rotunda

John Vanderlyn, *Landing of Columbus,* 1846.
ARCHITECT OF THE CAPITOL

in 1847, replete with a contritely bowing mutineer and a monk (though no monk was present on the voyage).

Among the several hundred poets to take on Columbus during the latter part of the nineteenth century were Ralph Waldo Emerson, Edward Everett Hall, and Alfred Tennyson. Walt Whitman has Columbus, on his deathbed, taking solace in a vision of the future when "anthems in new tongues I hear saluting me."

Because he was probably born in Genoa, Italian Americans especially idolized Columbus. In the second half of the nineteenth century, celebrations were held in many cities to which Italians had immigrated. In 1893, the World's Columbian Exposition drew an estimated twenty-seven million people to Chicago for a celebration of American technological prowess and of the four hundredth anniversary of Columbus's landing (one year late). In 1934, after lobbying by the Knights of Columbus, Franklin Roosevelt proclaimed Columbus Day a national holiday.

The twentieth century brought more sensitivity to the devastating impact European colonizers had on Native Americans. By the five hundredth anniversary of the landing, celebrations had turned into commemorations, and for many Columbus had come to stand less for American genius and more for American imperialism. The twentieth century also brought much new scholarship to debunk the mythology surrounding Columbus. Yet to the extent he was still a symbol—whose actual life was still shrouded in mystery—Columbus remained in many ways a mythological figure.

A few words about what is probably the most famous rhyme about Columbus:

"In fourteen hundred ninety-two/Columbus sailed the ocean blue."

The rhyme is routinely attributed, even by Columbus scholars, to Winifred Sackville Stoner Jr. Stoner was a renowned child prodigy and poet whose collection, *Facts in Jingles*, was published in 1915 and consisted of poems she wrote between the ages of five and twelve. The Columbus rhyme appeared in a 1919 poem of Stoner's, "The History of the U.S."

But those lines were being used to implant the date 1492 in children's minds long before Stoner wrote her poem. Witness, for example, a story from an 1890 Kansas newspaper in which a girl named Mary complains she can never remember when Columbus discovered America. Her friend recites the lines, clearly already famous. Mary is delighted, and later in the evening her friend asks if she can still remember the date. "Of course I can," Mary replies somewhat indignantly:

In fourteen hundred ninety-three
Columbus sailed the dark blue sea.

CHAPTER TWO

The Indian Princess

A FEW MORE THAN A HUNDRED YEARS AFTER COLUMBUS LANDED IN America and a few months after the British established their colony at Jamestown in 1607, Captain John Smith led a trading party up the Chickahominy River. He was captured by Indians and brought before Powhatan, who ruled over much of the region. Smith, writing in the third person for his *Generall Historie of Virginia, New England, and The Summer Isles*, described how the Indians dragged him before their emperor, Powhatan. The Indians were "ready with their clubs to beat out his brains." Luckily, "Pocahontas, the king's dearest daughter, . . . got his head in her arms, and laid her own upon his to save him from death."

This was not the only time Pocahontas saved the day. Pocahontas, Smith reported, visited Jamestown regularly. Soon after the rescue, when the colonists were starving, she brought food to Jamestown. Later, she warned Smith of an impending Indian attack. Without Pocahontas, the Virginia colony might very well not have survived a year, let alone become England's first foothold in America.

How did the Jamestown colonists reward Pocahontas? They kidnapped her.

In 1614, Captain Samuel Argall was sailing the Potomac River and learned that Pocahontas was nearby. He pressured an Indian named Iopassus to lure Pocahontas on board. Iopassus pretended his wife wanted to see the ship, and Pocahontas joined them. Iopassus and his wife then left; Pocahontas was forced to stay and then taken to Jamestown. A messenger was sent to Powhatan informing him, the colony's secretary reported, that his daughter would "be kept til such time as he would ransom her."

When Powhatan and the colonists could not agree on a ransom, the colonists decided to keep Pocahontas and convert her to Christianity. She was moved up the James River to Henrico and baptized as Rebecca. At Henrico she met John Rolfe, a colonist who decided to marry her. Rolfe wrote Virginia governor Thomas Dale asking permission. Rolfe stressed he was doing so "for the glory of God, for my own salvation, and for the converting to the knowledge of God and Jesus Christ an unbelieving creature, namely Pocahontas." Lest anyone suspect he was motivated by "carnal affection," Rolfe added he could easily have married "Christians more pleasing to the eye." The governor approved the marriage.

Two years later, in 1616, Pocahontas—now Rebecca—traveled with her husband and son to England. She joined the king and queen for a performance at court and met with the Bishop of London. She "still carried herself as the daughter of a king," according to one eyewitness. She had a brief reunion with John Smith just outside of London.

Smith reported in the *Generall Historie* that at this meeting Pocahontas was cold to him. "They did tell us always you were dead, and I knew no other till I came to Plymouth," Pocahontas said to Smith. "Powhatan did command . . . to seek you and know the truth, because your countrymen lie much."

Soon after, Pocahontas became ill and died. Rolfe returned to Virginia without her.

So ended the story of Pocahontas, at least as told by the Englishmen who were there (and we have no written accounts from Pocahontas or any other Indian). But from the start, there were doubters.

Smith's *Generall Historie*, the original source of the rescue story, did not instill confidence. Smith told some remarkable—many would say incredible—tales. Pocahontas, Smith wrote, was just one of four foreign ladies who, unable to resist Smith's charms, came to his aid. Before coming to Virginia, Smith had joined Austrian armies fighting against the Turks in Hungary. He was captured by the Turks and made a slave in Constantinople. There, "the beauteous Lady Tragabigzanda . . . did all she could," including sending him to her brother in Tartary, from where he escaped. He ultimately reached a Russian garrison where "the charitable Lady Callamata supplied my necessities." Later, when Smith escaped some pirates, "the good Lady Madam Chanoyes bountifully assisted me."

All this about a short and battle-scarred man whose portraits are distinctly underwhelming. No wonder some of Smith's contemporaries called him a braggart and a liar. But say this for Smith: At no point did he claim that Pocahontas rescued him because she loved him. At no point did he claim that Pocahontas wanted to marry him and not Rolfe. Pocahontas was about ten or eleven years old when—or if—she threw herself between Smith and the clubs of her father's warriors. She could conceivably have had a girlish crush on Smith, but the stories of the love between the brave captain and the beautiful princess could not be attributed to Smith.

The first to suggest this might be a love story was a Frenchman.

The Marquis de Chastellux visited Virginia in 1782 and recounted the story of Pocahontas as it was told to him. Rather than taking Smith's head in her arms, as Smith put it, Chastellux's Pocahontas "threw herself upon his body." When reunited with Smith outside London, she "threw herself into his arms" and, when he did not respond with equal passion, she "wept bitterly."

Still, Chastellux merely hinted at a love story and his Pocahontas was only twelve—probably a bit older than in actuality but still young. It was John Davis, an Englishman, who made her fourteen and turned this into a full-blown romance. In his *Travels of Four Years and a Half in the United States of America 1798, 1799, 1800, 1801, and 1802*, published in 1803, when Pocahontas first sees Smith she is immediately smitten. "Never did the moon gaze more steadfastly on the water," Davis wrote, "than she on the prisoner."

Smith, according to Davis, did not share these feelings, but he saw in Pocahontas an opportunity to advance the interests of the colony. For these he readily tolerated it when, as the two wandered along the banks of the river, "she gave loose to all the tumultuous ecstasy of love." Ever the gentleman, Smith returned to England and arranged for Pocahontas to be told he was dead. This created an opening for Rolfe, who "possessed not the ambition of Smith [but] was infinitely more accessible to the softer emotions." Indeed, Davis's Rolfe wrote love poems, one of which concluded:

> Here as I pensive wander through the glade,
> I sigh and call upon my Indian maid.

Soon after writing these words, "the impassioned youth clasped the Indian maid to his beating heart, and drank from her lips the poison of delight." As for Pocahontas, she had not forgotten Smith but was open to Rolfe's love. As Davis explained, "The breast of a woman is, perhaps, never more susceptible of a new passion than when it is agitated by the remains of a former one."

Thus did Davis turn what he called "the broken fragment which is to be found in the meager page of Chastellux" into a great romance. So enamored was Davis of the story that he expanded and further fictionalized it in two other works: *Captain Smith and Princess Pocahontas, An Indian Tale* and *The First Settlers of Virginia, An Historical Novel*. Both were published in 1805.

The evidence for a romance between Smith and Pocahontas remained flimsy. The playwright John Brougham, in his 1855 parody, *Po-ca-hon-tas, or The Gentle Savage*, poked fun at those who took the story seriously. Brougham described his work as "An Original Aboriginal Erratic Operatic Semi-Civilized and Demi-Savage Extravaganza, being a Per-Version of Ye Trewe and Wonderfulle Hystorie of Ye Renownned Princesse." He introduces Pocahontas as "the beautiful, and very properly undutiful daughter of King Pow-Ha-Tan, married, according to the ridiculous dictum of actual circumstance, to Master Rolff, but the author flatters himself much more advantageously disposed of [in this play]."

The play was a hit.

Pocahontas was no joking matter for many who took their Virginia ancestry seriously. Nor did these Virginia gentlemen and gentlewomen see any irony in claiming to be descended from an Indian while also expressing horror at any mention of mixing white and black blood.

Among those to put Pocahontas on a pedestal was George Washington Parke Custis, the step-grandson of George Washington. Custis's

1830 play, *Pocahontas, or the Settlers of Virginia*, presented a dignified heroine, as befitted the woman whose descendants prided themselves on being members of the "First Families of Virginia." There is no hint of lust in Custis's Pocahontas. Her rescue of Smith appears to be motivated by her Christianity—this despite the fact that in Smith's account she had at the time of the rescue not yet met any Christian. As Smith's would-be executioners raise their clubs and just before Pocahontas throws herself on Smith's body, she addresses her father: "Cruel king, the ties of blood which bound me to thee are dissever'd, . . . for know that I have abjur'd thy senseless gods, and now worship the Supreme Being."

Similarly, neither lust nor love motivates Pocahontas in Charlotte Barnes's 1848 play, *The Forest Princess, or Two Centuries Ago*. Rather, this Pocahontas is driven by a desire to see Indians and whites live in peace, even if it means her people have to give up their land and culture. In the play's final scene, Pocahontas has a vision. She sees Powhatan on the banks of the James River, awaiting her return. Then the allegorical figures of Time and Peace pass by, and in the distance she sees George Washington. She awakes and exclaims, "'tis no dream!"

Barnes's mother Mary, incidentally, starred in Custis's *Pocahontas*.

In paintings and sculptures, too, Pocahontas veered from a forest nymph to a dignified and pious woman. The two versions were there from the start: Smith's *Generall Historie* includes illustrations of a half-nude young Pocahontas rescuing Smith and also a portrait of "Lady Rebecca." (The latter, an engraving by Simon Van de Passe, was supposedly copied from a portrait made during her visit to England, and so may come closer than any other to her actual looks.) The image of Rebecca pushed aside that of Pocahontas in 1840, when John Gadsby Chapman's painting, *The Baptism of Pocahontas*, took its place in the Rotunda of the Capitol in Washington.

Chapman chose the scene, he explained, because it "addresses itself to all Christian people and Christian churches." Pocahontas "stands foremost in the train of those wandering children of the forest who have . . . been snatched from the fangs of a barbarous idolatry to become lambs in the fold of the Divine Shepherd." It's possible, however, that Chapman also preferred to paint the baptism instead of the rescue because the

John Gadsby Chapman, *The Baptism of Pocahontas*, 1840.
ARCHITECT OF THE CAPITOL

former was a fresher subject. Antonio Cappellano's 1825 relief, *Preservation of Captain Smith by Pocahontas*, was already displayed in the Capitol, and Chapman himself had already painted the rescue.

For Americans fulfilling what they saw as their manifest destiny, Pocahontas's embrace of Christianity—or for that matter of John Rolfe or John Smith—offered a soothing perspective on how the land was being cleared for white settlers. Pocahontas was a "good Indian." Had other Indians chosen to live among whites and take on white ways, violence might have been and might still be averted. True, the marriage to Rolfe raised uncomfortable feelings about miscegenation, especially among southerners uncomfortable with black-white relations. But the marriage of Pocahontas and Rolfe could, as Custis's Powhatan puts it, "be a pledge of the future union between England and Virginia." Looking further into the future, Custis's Powhatan saw "a long line of descendants [and] the time when these wild regions shall become the ancient and honour'd part of a great and glorious American Empire."

As the Civil War approached, Pocahontas's position as a symbol of American unity was undercut by the increasing tensions between North and South, for Pocahontas was very much a symbol of the South. She came from what would become Virginia, and Virginians claimed her as their own. In "A Dream of the Cavaliers," the Virginia poet John Esten Cooke had this to say of Smith and Pocahontas:

> And now in the light of glory
> The noble figures stand—
> The founder of Virginia,
> And the pride of Southern land!

Northerners, especially New Englanders, had their own story of where the nation was founded—at Plymouth Rock, by the Pilgrims—and how whites and good Indians came together—for the first Thanksgiving. New Englanders could not claim Plymouth came first: Jamestown was founded in 1607 and Plymouth in 1620. But New Englanders found plenty of holes to poke into Smith's story.

Among those to call Smith a liar was Henry Adams, the great-grandson of John Adams and the grandson of John Quincy Adams. Both presidents proudly hailed from Massachusetts. Henry Adams described Smith's *Generall Historie* as "remarkable for a curious air of exaggeration." More specifically and damningly, Adams placed side by side Smith's passages about his capture in his 1608 work, *A True Relation of Such Occurrences and Accidents of Noate as Hath Hapned in Virginia*, and those in the 1624 *Generall Historie*. The earlier work made no mention of Pocahontas saving him. For Adams, the reason was clear: Smith waited to publish the story until those who could have refuted it—including Pocahontas herself—were dead.

Virginians rose to Smith's defense. Cooke published a novel, *My Lady Pokahontas*, and William Wirt Henry, a lawyer and historian, took a more legalistic approach. Not coincidentally, Henry was the grandson of Virginia's Patrick Henry. In general, though, the southerners' view was losing out. Abraham Lincoln's 1863 proclamation that Thanksgiving would be a national holiday seemed to solidify the position of the Pilgrims as America's founding story.

"The story of one Indian girl's bravery," wrote art historian Ann Uhry Abrams, "could hardly compete with an entire army of self-righteous pilgrims."

Pocahontas's story never entirely faded from American memory. Advertisers continued to use her name to pitch everything from tobacco to bourbon to cleaning products. There was at least some logic to the tobacco ads, since Rolfe's experiments with growing sweeter strains of tobacco had been key to the Virginia colony's profitability. Bourbon was a bit more of a stretch. A 1987 ad for Old Grand-Dad suggested that, since the Indians introduced corn to the settlers and since corn is key to bourbon: "Next time you pour a finger of Old Grand-Dad, toast a great little lady, Pocahontas." As for cleansers: A 1952 ad had Pocahontas cleaning a sink in a tepee while Smith is about to be killed by Indians. Fortunately, Bab-O—the "world's sudsiest cleanser"—lets her finish the job in time to save Smith.

Musicians also kept alive the romance of Pocahontas. Peggy Lee's rendition of "Fever" sold millions and included lyrics about Romeo and Juliet—and about the "very mad affair" of Pocahontas and John Smith. Elvis Presley, Madonna, and Beyoncé also recorded the song.

Meanwhile, Smith's credibility was taking a turn for the better. Bradford Smith's 1953 biography of Smith included an appendix on the captain's Hungarian adventures written by Laura Striker Polanyi. Polanyi carefully checked Smith's narrative of the wars against the Turks. To almost everyone's surprise, everything that could be checked turned out to be accurate.

The case for Smith was further strengthened by ethnohistorians. Their work showed that Smith's descriptions of Indian life and culture were realistic. Many historians have concluded the "rescue" may have been part of a traditional ritual of death and rebirth that accompanied adoption into an Indian tribe. So Smith may have described the proceedings accurately; he just didn't understand what was really going on.

Dependent as we still are on Smith's storytelling, it is perhaps inevitable that we can't know for sure what was really going on in Pocahontas's mind. Did she love John Rolfe? Was she a traitor to her people—abandoning them to become English and Christian? Or did she give up her way of life to bring about peace, or perhaps to infiltrate an enemy world in the hope that what she learned might somehow save her people?

Sometimes it seems as if we haven't made any progress in understanding Pocahontas. When Donald Trump repeatedly called Senator Elizabeth Warren "Pocahontas," he surely didn't care about either the real Pocahontas or any of her mythic descendants. Trump was making fun of Warren's claim to Indian ancestry, and he seized on the name of the first and probably the only Indian woman who came to mind.

And Pocahontas's two most recent major movie appearances both focused on her fictional romance with Smith. Disney's 1995 animated *Pocahontas* owed more to the fantasies told to and by the Marquis de Chastellux than it did to the histories of John Smith, let alone the actual history of Pocahontas. Pocahontas was, again, a sexy Indian princess.

"Pocahontas is suddenly part of Barbie's culture," wrote Martina Whelshula and Faith Spotted Eagle, both Native Americans. "A culture where a girl heroine lives only for approval from men. In this case, John Smith." Terrence Malick's 2005 *The New World*, which starred Q'orianka Kilcher as Pocahontas, was also criticized as sexist.

But both movies allowed some historical truth to prevail by having John Rolfe and not John Smith marry Pocahontas, though in Disney's case it wasn't until the 1998 sequel. And both movies portrayed Pocahontas's people positively, if not always accurately.

Irene Bedard, the Native American actress Disney cast for the voice of Pocahontas, defended the movie. "I grew up being called Pocahontas, a derogatory term. They hissed that name at me, as if it was something dirty. Now . . . Pocahontas can reach a large culture as a heroine.

"No, it doesn't make up for five hundred years of genocide," Bedard continued. But "when I was growing up, I wanted so much to be Barbie. Now, some little girl might want to be Pocahontas."

CHAPTER THREE

Giving Thanks

IN THE FALL OF 1621, A YEAR AFTER ARRIVING IN MASSACHUSETTS, THE Pilgrims celebrated their harvest. This was, the traditional tale goes, the first Thanksgiving. "Now began to come in a store of fowl, as winter approached," wrote William Bradford, governor of the Plymouth colony, "And besides waterfowl there was great store of wild turkeys, of which they took many."

Another colonist, Edward Winslow, added that at the fall feast they were joined by many Indians, "whom for three days we entertained and feasted."

So: There was turkey. There were Indians. But: No cranberry sauce. No pumpkin pie. And, contrary to our image of God-thanking Pilgrims, no mention of "thanksgiving." You can find on various Christian websites a proclamation in which Bradford, as governor, calls on "all ye Pilgrims with your wives and little ones" to gather and "render Thanksgiving to the Almighty God," but this appears to be a twentieth-century invention. No Pilgrim primary source ties Thanksgiving to the 1621 feast or to any fall feast.

The people we know as Pilgrims were known in their own time as Separatists. The Puritans, as their name implied, wanted to purify the Church of England of papist practices, because they thought the Protestant Reformation had not gone far enough. The Separatists, as *their* name implied, wanted to go even further; they wanted not to reform the church but to separate from it entirely. Bradford and other members of a Separatist congregation left England for Holland, where there was more religious freedom. But Holland presented problems of its own—an absence of good jobs and, as Bradford put it, "the evil examples" that were drawing some Pilgrim children "into extravagant and dangerous courses." So, strange as it may seem to us, many of the Pilgrims came to America not because of any missionary zeal but because they thought life would be easier than in Holland.

Moreover, of the 102 passengers who departed for America on the *Mayflower* in September 1620, fewer than half were members of Bradford's Separatist congregation. The rest had been recruited either by the Separatists or by the London investors supporting the venture. These "strangers," as Bradford called them, set out for America with no religious motivations whatsoever.

Still, those debunkers who would deny any connection between the Pilgrims and giving thanks go too far. As Christians, Pilgrims routinely thanked God. In 1623, when rains followed a damaging drought, Bradford reported the colonists "set apart a day of thanksgiving." At their fall feast, they probably gave thanks to God, just as plenty of other Spanish and French and English colonists in America undoubtedly did before and after 1621.

What the Pilgrims did *not* do was declare their harvest festival a day of Thanksgiving.

Historians looking for a more official date for a first Thanksgiving might settle on 1777 when, after American and French troops defeated the British at Saratoga, the Continental Congress proclaimed a day of thanksgiving. Or there are various days of thanksgiving George Washington, John Adams, and James Madison declared during their presidencies. Thomas Jefferson thought these threatened the separation of church and state and did not declare any days of thanksgiving, but he need not have worried. None of these presidential decrees led to any sort of national tradition or holiday.

It was not until 1841 that Alexander Young, in a collection of the works of Bradford and Winslow and other Pilgrims, called the 1621 feast "the first Thanksgiving." And it was not until 1846 that Sara Josepha Hale, editor of a magazine called *Godey's Lady's Book*, began campaigning, in editorials and letters to government officials, to make Thanksgiving a national holiday. (Hale was also a poet. Her most famous work begins, "Mary had a little lamb.")

The case for a national Thanksgiving holiday gained momentum in 1856 when Bradford's book, *On Plymouth Plantation*, was published in its entirety. Parts of the book had been published earlier in other works, including Young's, but the full manuscript had been thought lost until it was found in 1855 in the library of the Bishop of London. How it ended up there remains a mystery.

In 1863, not long after Hale had written directly to Abraham Lincoln, her long campaign paid off. Lincoln proclaimed the last Thursday of November "as a day of Thanksgiving and praise to our beneficent Father." Lincoln expressed gratitude that the Union armies and navies were advancing and that, in the midst of the Civil War, "harmony has prevailed everywhere except in the theater of military conflict." He did not mention the Pilgrims.

In New England, however, the Pilgrims were in the front and center of American history, and it was often the Mayflower Compact that put them there. The Compact, declared the historian George Bancroft (whose ancestors had arrived in Massachusetts in 1632), was the "birth of popular constitutional liberty."

The Compact was signed in November 1620 off the coast of Cape Cod, a few weeks before the Pilgrims settled on Plymouth as the site of their colony. The signers agreed to "combine ourselves together into a civil body politic" and to "constitute and frame such just and equal laws, ordinances, acts, constitutions and offices . . . as shall be thought most meet and convenient for the general good of the colony."

In 1802, speaking at the anniversary of the Pilgrims' landing, John Quincy Adams called the document "perhaps the only instance, in human history, of that positive, original social compact, which speculative philosophers have imagined as the only legitimate source of government." Adams—as a member of a Massachusetts presidential dynasty and in 1802 already a member of the state senate—was eager to place the birth of American democracy off the coast of what would become his state.

Jamestown had preceded Plymouth, he conceded, but those Virginia settlers had been motivated by "avarice and ambition." It was the Pilgrims, Adams clearly implied, who with the Mayflower Compact set America on the course of democracy.

Adams conveniently ignored the fact that the Mayflower Compact began with an affirmation of loyalty to the king and that, according to Bradford himself, the Separatists drew up the Compact as a means of controlling the rebellious "strangers." Besides, as many debunkers of Pilgrim mythology have pointed out, plenty of English towns had local governments based on similar compacts. Still, Adams was right to see that the Compact mattered: It established a government based on "assent by all the individuals of the community," and it did so an ocean away from any English precedents.

There was less of a case for exalting Plymouth Rock— on which the Pilgrims supposedly stepped ashore. *Mourt's Relation*, a booklet written by Bradford and Winslow that was published in England in 1622, describes how the Pilgrims found at Plymouth "a very good harbor," and then "marched also into the land, and found diverse cornfields, and little running brooks."

Not a word of a rock—either in *Mourt's Relation* or in Bradford's *Of Plymouth Plantation*. In fact, the rock did not appear in print until more than two hundred years after the Pilgrims landed. According to James Thacher's 1832 history of Plymouth, the story was passed down by an "Elder Faunce," who around 1741 heard that a wharf was to be built over the rock. This "impressed his mind with deep concern." Wanting to see the rock one more time, the ninety-five-year-old Faunce was carried from his home to the waterfront. He pointed to the rock; this was where, Faunce's father had assured him, the Pilgrims first stepped ashore. Faunce then "bedewed it with his tears."

Thacher's third-hand account is as close as we can come to a landing on Plymouth Rock. Still, the story Faunce told *might* be true. The Pilgrims might have seen a rock as a steadier step than the surrounding beach. The authors of *Mourt's Relation* and *Of Plymouth Plantation* left out plenty of other details and had no way to know this particular one would come to matter.

In any case, as revolution approached, the rock became a near-sacred symbol of America's origins. Since a pier had been built over the rock, in 1774 the inhabitants of Plymouth decided to move the rock to a place where it could be better honored. Thacher described how the villagers assembled with about thirty yoke of oxen. But as they tried to raise the rock onto a carriage, it split apart. The quick-thinking patriots of Plymouth decided, Thacher recounted, that "the separation of the rock was . . . ominous of a division of the British empire."

That the rock was now broken in two—with half moved to the town square and the other half still by the water— in no way dampened the celebrations surrounding it. At the two hundredth anniversary of the landing, Daniel Webster, not yet a senator but already a famed orator, spoke of the rock as the first step toward the nation's manifest destiny. "'If God prosper us,' might have been the . . . language of our Fathers, when they landed upon this Rock," said Webster, "'we shall here begin a work which shall last for ages, we shall plant here a new society, in the principles of the fullest liberty, and the purest religion; we shall subdue this wilderness which is before us; we shall fill this region of the great continent, which stretches almost from pole to pole with the civilization and Christianity.'"

Samuel Morse, who became famous for his part in inventing the telegraph, was earlier well known as an artist and in 1811 painted *Landing of the Forefathers*. For decades, Morse lobbied for a Pilgrim painting of his to go in the Capitol in Washington, DC, but that commission went instead to Robert Walter Weir, whose *Embarkation of the Pilgrims* was unveiled in 1843. Morse's desire to honor the Pilgrims was motivated in part by his hatred of Catholics and immigrants, who he believed were undermining the forefathers' legacy. Indeed, his nativist diatribes may have undermined his case to have his work in the Capitol.

It was not just nativists who claimed the Rock as their starting point. "The rock underlies all America," said the abolitionist Wendell Phillips in 1855. "It has cropped out a great many times in our history. . . . Old Putnam stood upon it at Bunker Hill . . . Jefferson had it for a writing-desk when he drafted the Declaration of Independence . . . Garrison had it for an imposing stone when he looked in the faces of seventeen millions of angry men."

In 1880, the two parts of the rock were reunited on the waterfront and protected by a fence. By then, though, at least some Americans looked on it with less reverence. "The Pilgrims were a simple and ignorant race," said Mark Twain in 1881. "They never had seen any good rocks before, . . . and so they were excusable for hopping ashore in frantic delight and clapping an iron fence around this one."

Among the silliest of the questions that swirled around the rock was who was the first Pilgrim to step on it. The claimants were Mary Chilton and John Alden, and their descendants spent a great deal of energy supporting their respective claims. Even James Thacher, who did not hesitate to accept the Elder Faunce's account of the Rock, concluded that "the point of precedence must remain undecided, since the closest investigation discloses no authority nor a shadow of evidence in favor of any individual as being the first who landed." William S. Russell, like Thacher a resident historian of Plymouth, tried to satisfy both parties by suggesting that a chivalrous Alden might have "yielded his claim to the lady."

Alden's chivalry was key to one of the most widespread myths about a Pilgrim. This was the love triangle between Alden, Myles Standish, and Priscilla Mullins.

Standish was the military leader of the Pilgrims. Before leaving for America, the Pilgrims had been in touch with John Smith, who had not only led the Jamestown settlers in Virginia but had also explored New England. The Pilgrims chose Standish instead. Standish lacked Smith's experience, especially when it came to negotiating with Indians, but he led a number of successful defenses and attacks against them. His courage in battle did not extend to romance, however, so when he fell in love with Mullins he sent Alden, who himself secretly loved Mullins, to approach her on his behalf. At the time Standish was in his late twenties or early thirties, Alden was twenty-one, and Mullins was seventeen.

The earliest printed version of the story came from Timothy Alden, a descendant of John's, in 1814. John Alden first spoke on Standish's behalf to Mullins's father and then to Mullins herself according to Timothy Alden, who continued:

John Alden, who is said to have been a man of most excellent form with a fair and ruddy complexion, . . . delivered his errand. Miss Mullins listened with respectful attention, and at last, after a considerable pause, fixing her eyes upon him, with an open and pleasant countenance, said, "prithee, John, why do you not speak for yourself?"

Henry Wadsworth Longfellow's epic poem, *The Courtship of Miles Standish*, made immortal Priscilla's words, in Wadsworth's version: "Why don't you speak for yourself, John?" Longfellow, like Timothy Alden, was a descendant of John Alden.

Actually, Longfellow did not quite succeed in making Alden's line immortal, since Longfellow's poems fell out of the canon and schoolchildren no longer had to memorize his lines. But as late as the 1950s the John Alden brand of vegetables came with a slogan on the can saying it speaks for itself.

In the poem, Alden and Mullins marry but only after they receive a mistaken report that Standish has been killed in a battle with the Indians. Standish appears just as the ceremony is over and forgives them both.

There's no evidence of the love triangle in any of the Pilgrim primary sources. Plymouth records do, however, confirm that John and Priscilla were married, that Myles Standish found another bride, and that their son Alexander Standish later married Sarah Alden, the daughter of John and Priscilla.

As a military leader, Standish was brutal and often effective. But the Pilgrims' success in establishing peace with Indians had less to do with military victories and more to do with the weaknesses of both the settlers and the nearby Pokanonet people.

Among the first Indians to greet the settlers was Tisquantum, whom the Pilgrims called Squanto. In 1614, six years before the Pilgrims arrived, Squanto had been kidnapped by Englishmen who explored the region under John Smith. Squanto arrived in London, where he learned English and may even have learned of the Separatists' plans to come to America before himself returning with an English explorer. Squanto introduced the Pilgrims to Massasoit, the leader—or sachem—of the Pokanonets.

Massasoit was in an extremely vulnerable position. His people had been decimated by a disease brought to America by earlier European fishermen and for which the Native Americans had no antibodies. A few years earlier, Massasoit had commanded thousands of warriors; by the time the Pilgrims arrived he was down to a few hundred. Neighboring tribes had not been hit as hard by the disease and were threatening to invade Pokanonet territory and topple Massasoit.

The Pilgrims, too, were vulnerable. Despite their superior weapons, they needed the Indians' knowledge. Squanto, for example, taught them how to grow corn successfully by fertilizing the soil with dead fish.

And so the Pokanonet and Pilgrims agreed to an alliance that, though often uneasy, lasted more than fifty years. By then, English settlements had greatly expanded and pushed the Indians out of their territory. In 1675 Massasoit's son, Metacom, waged a desperate and unsuccessful war to stem the English tide. Metacom was known to the English as Philip and the war, in which the Indians were soundly defeated, was known as King Philip's War. No wonder, then, that in 1970 some Native Americans declared Thanksgiving a day of mourning.

But back in 1621, at the fall festival that mistakenly came to be seen as the first Thanksgiving, Massasoit was definitely an ally and probably present. Certainly other Indians were present and indeed outnumbered the Pilgrims. The Pilgrims may very well have thanked them, as well as God, for their survival.

Lydia Maria Child, a nineteenth-century campaigner for women's rights and human rights, wrote a novel in 1824, *Hobomok*, set during King Philip's War. But the reality of Indian wars was not what Americans wanted to remember about Thanksgiving Day, so it's not surprising that Child's best-known work is "A New England Boy's Thanksgiving," a poem still familiar today:

> Over the river, and through the wood,
>   To grandfather's house we go;

J. L. G. Ferris, *The First Thanksgiving 1621,* between 1900 and 1920.
LIBRARY OF CONGRESS

The horse knows the way,
To carry the sleigh,
Through the white and drifted snow.
Over the river, and through the wood,
To grandfather's house away!
We would not stop
For doll or top,
For 'tis Thanksgiving Day.

Child was certainly not alone in cutting Native Americans out of the Thanksgiving story. At Macy's Thanksgiving parades, held since 1924, a cartoon-like and stereotypical Indian appeared in a 1939 balloon, but generally the balloons are the likes of Mickey Mouse and Kermit the Frog.

And what of the most prevalent of today's Thanksgiving rituals?

Well, neither Bradford nor Winslow mentioned football, and the Separatists, like the Puritans, didn't approve of ball games. True, Edward

Winslow, in his letter from Plymouth describing the first harvest, did say that "amongst other recreations, we exercised our guns," but he didn't specify what those other recreations were and football, at least in anything resembling its current form, didn't exist until the late nineteenth century.

But football and Thanksgiving did go together from football's earliest days. In 1876, the year four Ivy League universities formed the Intercollegiate Football Association, the final was held on Thanksgiving. By 1893, the *New York Herald* wrote: "Thanksgiving is no longer a solemn festival to God for mercies given. It is a holiday granted by the State and the Nation to see a game of football."

Indians still lurk somewhere in the background of our collective Thanksgiving memories, however. A 2014 *New Yorker* cover by Bruce McCall shows Indians and Pilgrims about to share a dinner with a football game on TV. And what team is playing?

The Washington Redskins.

CHAPTER FOUR

The Jolly Roger

UNLIKE THE PILGRIMS, WHOSE STORIES DID NOT SPREAD FAR AND WIDE until long after their alleged landing at Plymouth Rock, pirates were very much legends in their own time. Partly this was the pirates' own doing: The more a pirate captain cultivated a fearsome image, the more likely it was that the ships he attacked would quickly surrender—and the more likely his own crew would follow his orders.

Blackbeard understood the value of a ruthless image. Once, while drinking in his cabin with two crewmembers, he suddenly shot one of them—his pilot, Israel Hands—through the knee. Asked why he did so, Blackbeard explained "that if he did not now and then kill one of them, they would forget who he was."

That story was recounted by Captain Charles Johnson, author of *A General History of the Robberies and Murders of the Most Notorious Pirates.* Pirates eager to spread their notoriety could have found no better chronicler than Johnson. The book first appeared in 1724, when sailors and coastal residents were much worried by pirates. If they read Johnson's book and then spotted the skull and crossbones of a pirate flag, they were all the more terrified.

Johnson's colorful descriptions of pirates set the tone for centuries. Of Blackbeard, Johnson wrote, "he assumed the cognomen . . . from that large quantity of hair which, like a frightful meteor, covered his whole face and frightened America more than any comet that has appeared there a long time."

"In time of action," Johnson continued, "he wore a sling over his shoulders with three brace of pistols hanging in holsters like bandoliers, and stuck lighted matches under his hat, which, appearing on each side of his face, his eyes naturally looking fierce and wild, made him altogether such a figure, that imagination cannot form an idea of a fury, from hell, to look more frightful."

It's unclear what ship, if any, Captain Johnson captained, but he clearly knew a lot about pirate life. He may have lived with pirates at some point, or interviewed them, or perhaps studied transcripts of pirate trials. Among those he may have met was Israel Hands, who survived Blackbeard's shot (though from then on he walked with a limp) and who Johnson described as "alive at this time in London, begging his bread."

Other contemporary sources, such as trial transcripts and newspaper accounts, have shown that the *General History* is generally accurate. But Johnson was certainly not above adding colorful details—details which others would later repeat and expand upon.

Captain William Kidd did not have to wait for Johnson to immortalize him in print. The day Kidd was hanged—May 23, 1701—a ballad was sung about him and it may even have been printed and sold in time for the execution. The ballad has since appeared in various forms; the following excerpts are from a version printed in Boston sometime between 1810 and 1814 and titled "The Dying Words of Capt. Robert Kidd." (It's not clear why some balladeers in the century after Kidd's death changed his name from William to Robert.)

> My name was Robert Kidd, and God's law I did forbid,
>   And so wickedly I did when I sail'd. . . .
> I'd a bible in my hand, by my father's great command,
>   But I sunk it in the sand when I sail'd. . . .
> Come all you young and old, you're welcome to my gold,
>   For by it I've lost my soul, and must die. . . .

Contrary to the dying words in the ballad, Kidd went to the gallows proclaiming his innocence, and though he was by no means guiltless, he was to some extent a victim of politics. Even his prosecutors agreed Kidd had at one point been a privateer. Like pirates, privateers robbed ships at sea, but with a big difference: They were licensed by one nation, and they could only attack the ships of hostile nations. Kidd's privateering expedition was sponsored by leading figures in England's ruling Whig Party, including the Earl of Bellomont.

After wandering about the coasts of Africa and Asia and finding only a few small vessels, Kidd and his crew got itchy and seized a ship with an English captain. Kidd insisted it was a French ship, the captain notwithstanding, and he arrived in Boston confident he would be protected by Bellomont, the newly appointed governor of Massachusetts. But Bellomont's Tory opponents saw a chance to embarrass the Whigs, and the governor wanted to avoid being involved in a scandal. So Bellomont shipped Kidd off to London to be tried.

Kidd, in short, was not a very successful pirate. His lasting contribution to pirate lore was the idea of buried treasure. Perhaps because he didn't fully trust Bellomont, before arriving in Boston Kidd left some gold and silver with John Gardiner of Gardiner's Island, off the coast of Long Island, and stories circulated that a fortune was buried there.

Alas, there was no buried treasure on Gardiner's Island. Gardiner didn't want to tangle with Bellomont, and after Kidd's arrest he turned what he had over to the governor. The rest of Kidd's loot probably ended up in the hands of his crew, many of whom had deserted long before he reached Boston. Those crewmembers, whether they were privateers or pirates, had signed up in the hope of getting rich, and it's hard to imagine they walked away empty-handed. And once they had the money in their hands, they were far more likely to spend it than to bury it.

Nonetheless, stories spread of fortunes Kidd—or some other pirate— had buried somewhere along the coast. In 1727 Benjamin Franklin noted the "odd humor of digging for money, through a belief that much has been hidden by pirates." Franklin complained "you can hardly walk half a mile out of the town on any side, without observing several pits dug with that design, and perhaps some lately opened." By 1876, Mark Twain could write in *Tom Sawyer*: "There comes a time in every rightly constructed boy's life when he has a raging desire to go somewhere and dig for buried treasure."

Washington Irving, so instrumental in enhancing Columbus legends, did much for Kidd's treasure as well. Kidd appears in a number of Irving's stories. In "The Devil and Tom Walker," Tom Walker makes a Faustian deal with the devil, who promises him Kidd's buried fortune. The story ends with the devil collecting Tom's soul.

There's a happier ending in Howard Pyle's "Tom Chist and the Treasure Box." An orphan boy, Tom Chist, lives along the Delaware Bay and witnesses Kidd and his men burying treasure in the sand sometime before the pirates headed to New York. Tom finds not only the treasure but also Kidd's records, which indicate the treasure belongs to the wealthy Richard Chillingsworth of New York. When the impeccably honest Tom goes to New York to return the treasure, he discovers he is Chillingsworth's long-lost nephew. So Tom Chist—or rather, Thomas Chillingsworth—"became rich and great, as was to be supposed."

But stories by Irving and Pyle and others, including Edgar Allan Poe, were clearly fiction. In reality, despite the effort of numerous treasure hunters—including companies founded solely to search—no one found any treasure of Kidd's.

Stories also placed Blackbeard's alleged buried treasure up and down the coast. For Blackbeard legends, Johnson again deserves part of the credit. According to Johnson, the night before Blackbeard was killed, as he waited to battle two ships intent on capturing him, the pirate captain sat up drinking with his men. One asked whether Blackbeard's wife knew where he had buried his money. Blackbeard's answer, Johnson wrote, was that "nobody but himself and the devil knew where it was and the longest liver should take all."

One supposed site of Blackbeard's treasure was Blackbeard Island, off the coast of Georgia and now a National Wildlife Refuge. The US Fish and Wildlife Service website notes: "Legends tell of his murderous and plunderous activities along the coast and his periodic retreats to the island for 'banking' purposes." The last serious hunt for Blackbeard's treasure on the island was in the 1880s, and "the hunters were unsuccessful

"Kidd at Gardiner's Island," from *Howard Pyle's Book of Pirates*, 1921.

despite the use of maps and a divining rod." The website reminds refuge visitors that artifact hunting is a federal violation.

Stories of buried treasure often mixed with ghost stories. John F. Watson collected volumes of reminiscences of earlier days and first published them in 1830. "An idea was very prevalent," Watson reported, "especially near the Delaware and Schuylkill waters, that the pirates of Black Beard's day had deposited treasure in the earth. The fancy was, that sometimes they killed a prisoner and interred him with it, to make his ghost keep his vigils there and guard it."

Blackbeard's death was grisly enough to generate all sorts of supernatural stories. Virginia's Governor Alexander Spotswood was fed up with Blackbeard's piracy and perhaps also eager to get his hands on some of Blackbeard's riches. Spotswood commissioned Lieutenant Robert Maynard to hunt down the pirate, and Maynard found Blackbeard anchored off Ocracoke Island near the North Carolina coast. On the morning of November 22, 1718, Maynard attacked.

"They were now closely and warmly engaged," Johnson wrote, "'till the sea was tinctured with blood round the vessel. Blackbeard received a shot into his body from the pistol that Lieutenant Maynard discharged, yet he stood his ground and fought with great fury." When Blackbeard finally fell, "the lieutenant caused Blackbeard's head to be severed from his body and hung up at the bowsprit end."

Blackbeard's head arrived in Virginia where according to Watson "the skull was made into the bottom part of a very large punch bowl . . . which was long used as a drinking vessel at the Raleigh Tavern in Williamsburg. It was enlarged with silver, or silver plated; and I have seen those whose forefathers have spoken of their drinking punch from it."

The skull-turned-drinking vessel also supposedly turned up on Ocracoke Island, near where Blackbeard was killed. A North Carolina judge, Charles Harry Whedbee, recalled how he and a fellow law student visited the island in the early 1930s when they were law students. They were admitted to a secret gathering (Whedbee's friend knew the password: "Death to Spotswood") where all drank from the cup.

"The oblate spheroid shape of the cup was due to the cup's being the silver-plated skull of Blackbeard himself," Whedbee wrote. "I became a little queasy when it dawned on me that, if the cup was a skull, then the little dips in its lip had to be the eye sockets!"

An alleged Blackbeard skull-cup also found its way into the collection of the esteemed Peabody-Essex Museum in Salem, Massachusetts, though the museum treats the story of its origins as folklore and not fact. The cup is still in the museum's collection but not currently on view.

Another museum associated with Blackbeard is Colonial Williamsburg, the restored eighteenth-century capital of Virginia. Visitors to the town's gaol are told, accurately, that this is where some members of Blackbeard's crew who survived the battle with Maynard were imprisoned. And a book published by Colonial Williamsburg includes, along with disclaimers making clear that the museum is not vouching for the story's accuracy, a tale of Blackbeard's courtship to the daughter of North Carolina's governor. Alas, this Miss Eden was in love with someone else—a young man named Phillip.

When Blackbeard appeared at Phillip's door, the young man is understandably frightened. "He knew who stood before him," the story goes. "Who wouldn't recognize that beast of a man with the mass of hair upon his face?"

Weeks later, Miss Eden is wondering why she hasn't heard from Phillip when she receives a package. She hopes Phillip has sent an engagement ring. But when she removes the wrapping, she finds, on a red pillow, Phillip's severed hand. There's also a note: "You wished for his hand . . . and now you have it."

Stories of women pirates, at least those Johnson told, had endings no happier than Miss Eden's.

Mary Read's mother first gave birth to a boy, according to Johnson. Both the boy and his father died. Then Mary was born, with a different father who abandoned mother and child. Mary's mother, in order to gain the support of the first father's family, pretended Mary was that first father's son. Hence Read was brought up as a boy, and she was thus well prepared later to dress and fight like a soldier and then a pirate. In general, she managed to conceal her gender until she fell in love with a man on board a pirate ship. Indeed, she was so in love that when her lover quarreled with one of the pirates, Read took it upon herself to challenge her lover's adversary. "She fought him at sword and pistol," Johnson wrote, "and killed him upon the spot."

Anne Bonny's equally convoluted story began with her father disguising her as a boy to conceal that this was the child he had had with the family's maid and not with his wife. Bonny eloped with a pirate captain, John Rackham, and it was clear she too was fit for the pirate life. Indeed, after Rackham was captured and just before he was to be executed, "all the comfort she gave him," Johnson reported, "was that she was sorry to see him there, but if he had fought like a man, he need not have been hanged like a dog."

Read and Bonny sailed together for a stretch. After they were captured, their crewmates testified "that in times of action, no person amongst them were more resolute, or ready to board or undertake anything that was hazardous." Both Read and Bonny escaped hanging because, as they revealed following their convictions, they were pregnant. Read died in prison soon after her trial; what happened to Bonny is unknown.

Given the potential for both drama and romance, it's surprising that the stories of Read and Bonny have not inspired more works. But the two have appeared in several books, plays, movies, and video games. And perhaps it's a sign that their time is coming that a band called The Baja Brigade recorded in 2018 "The Ballad of Mary Read and Anne Bonny."

One pirate tradition very much based in reality was marooning people on desert islands. Indeed, one of the reasons Maynard could defeat Blackbeard was because the pirate had recently marooned many of his crew on an island off the North Carolina coast. Blackbeard did so, Johnson explained, so he could keep the brunt of his loot for himself and those closest to him. Marooning usually meant a slow death on a sandy island with little food or shelter.

When most people think of a desert island, however, what comes to mind is anything but a desert; rather, it's a tropical paradise a la Gilligan's, or at least an island on which it's possible to survive. That's largely thanks to Daniel Defoe's 1719 novel, *Robinson Crusoe*. Crusoe is shipwrecked, not put ashore by pirates. But Defoe was inspired by the true story of Alexander Selkirk, who was marooned on an island off the coast of Chile after quarrelling with the captain of a privateering expedition. Selkirk was marooned for four years; Crusoe for twenty-eight.

Even more than *Robinson Crusoe*, the novel that shaped our image of pirates was Robert Louis Stevenson's 1883 *Treasure Island*. Stevenson did not invent treasure maps or tropical islands or pirates with wooden legs and parrots. He borrowed from Johnson and Irving and Defoe and others, and he also drew upon real pirates, mentioning Kidd and Blackbeard in the book and even including Israel Hands as a character. But Stevenson deserves the credit for pulling it all together into an unforgettable work and an especially unforgettable character, the jovial and ruthless Long John Silver. In various adaptations Silver was later played by Wallace Beery (1934), Robert Newton (1950), Orson Welles (1972), Anthony Quinn (1987), and Charlton Heston (1990).

As pirates like Blackbeard receded into history, some fictional pirates became clean-cut heroes, both noble and handsome. In movies like *The Black Pirate* (1926) and *Captain Blood* (1935), Douglas Fairbanks Sr. and Errol Flynn play swashbuckling Robin Hood types.

Fictional pirates also became more comic, as in *The Pirates of Penzance*, which opened in 1879. In Gilbert and Sullivan's opera, the pirates have a reputation for sparing the lives of orphans, so everyone they capture claims to be an orphan. As for the pirates, it turns out they are "all noblemen who have gone wrong."

The most famous comic pirate was, of course, the one whose hand was bitten off by a crocodile— Captain Hook of J. M. Barrie's *Peter Pan*, which was first produced as a play in 1904 and published as a novel in 1911. Hook has been played by, among others, Boris Karloff (1950), Tim Curry (1990), and Dustin Hoffman (1991).

And then there's Johnny Depp's Jack Sparrow of Disney's multibillion-dollar series, *Pirates of the Caribbean*. Sparrow was as comically threatening as Hook, though Depp, who appears to have immersed himself in the lives of both eighteenth-century pirates and twentieth-century rock stars, said he modeled the character on Keith Richards.

CHAPTER FIVE

The Cherry Tree

THE PILGRIMS MAY HAVE BEEN OUR FOREFATHERS, BUT THERE IS ONLY one Father of our Country. As early as January 1776, even before independence was declared, Levi Allen (the brother of the Revolutionary War hero Ethan) called George Washington "our political father and head of a great people." By the time Washington became president, his fatherhood was well established.

He is not the cuddling kind of father. On the Mall in Washington, DC, the monuments to Thomas Jefferson and Abraham Lincoln portray people; Washington's is a stone obelisk.

Washington himself was partly to blame. He went to great lengths to keep his feelings private. As Washington neared his retirement, the wife of the British minister told the president he looked happy. "You are wrong," Washington replied, "my countenance never yet betrayed my feelings."

"He is in our textbooks and our wallets," wrote his biographer Richard Brookhiser, "but not our hearts."

The first big effort to humanize Washington was that of the minister and traveling bookseller Mason Locke Weems. His 1800 *Life and Memorable Actions of George Washington* was a huge bestseller.

Weems made the young George especially endearing. This George was certainly more approachable than the one in Weems's main competitor, the five-volume *Life of Washington* written by Supreme Court chief justice John Marshall and published between 1804 and 1807. Marshall's young George was as cold as his adult version; indeed, the opening section of volume two was titled "The Birth of Mr. Washington."

To create an endearing young Washington took a lot of creativity on Weems's part, since virtually nothing was known of Washington's childhood. The most famous story of Washington's childhood did not appear until the fifth edition of Weems's book in 1806, then titled *Life of Washington*. As Weems told the story, the six-year-old George received a hatchet as a present and promptly started chopping everything in sight, including his father's favorite cherry tree.

> *The next morning the old gentleman . . . came into the house . . . Presently George and his hatchet made their appearance. George, said his father, do you know who killed that beautiful little cherry tree yonder in the garden? This was a tough question, and George staggered under it for a moment, but quickly recovered himself; and looking at his father, with the sweet face of youth brightened with the inexpressible charm of all-conquering truth, he bravely cried out, "I can't tell a lie, Pa; you know I can't tell a lie. I did cut it with my hatchet."*

His father embraced him, telling him he was glad he had killed the tree, since George's courageous honesty was "worth more than a thousand trees, though blossomed with silver, and their fruits of purest gold."

Weems claimed he had heard the story from a distant relative of the family who as a girl had spent much time with the Washingtons. That was hardly a verifiable source, and from the start there were skeptics. The 1800 edition of the *Monthly Magazine and American Review* called Weems's biography (and this was before Weems added the cherry tree story) "as entertaining and edifying matter as can be found in the annals of fanaticism and absurdity." Other early biographers, including Jared Sparks, whose work appeared between 1834 and 1837, and Washington Irving (1855–1859), made no mention of the cherry tree, and later ones were openly derisory. Wrote biographer William Roscoe Thayer in 1922: "Only those who willfully prefer to deceive themselves need waste time over an imaginary Father of His Country amusing himself with a fictitious cherry-tree and hatchet."

None of this slowed the spread of the cherry-tree story. William Holmes McGuffey, like Weems a minister, included the story in grammar school textbooks read by millions of children in the eighteenth century. In case any student might have missed the moral of the story, McGuffey's *Readers* included prompts: "When we have done wrong, what are we tempted to do?" And: "What may we expect by confessing our faults?"

In an 1864 version of the story, Washington's father is about to punish a slave for cutting the cherry tree. George arrives just in time. "'Oh, papa, papa,' cried he, 'don't whip poor Jerry; if somebody must be whipped, let it be me, for it was I, and not Jerry, that cut the cherry tree.'" George's father embraces George, a la Weems, and Jerry is also grateful.

The "honesty-is-the-best-policy" moral could also be drawn from a story told by Martha Washington's grandson, George Washington Parke Custis. (George and Martha had no children together, probably because the father of his country was sterile.) Custis recounted how young George tried to tame a horse that was his mother's favorite but that was too fierce to ride. George and the horse were equally willful, and their struggle ended only when the horse "burst his noble heart" and died. Young George confessed to his mother, who at first was angry but quickly softened and said: "I rejoice in my son, who always speaks the truth."

Custis's stories of George's youth often highlighted his physical strength and prowess. The story that he threw a silver dollar across the Potomac River originated with Custis's tale of a rock thrown across the Rappahannock River at Fredericksburg. (Custis said it was a piece of slate about the size and shape of a dollar.)

Was Custis credible? Well, Washington really was very strong, and he was a talented horseman and had a powerful arm as both boy and man. And Custis spent much of his childhood at Mount Vernon and had access to other relatives' recollections. Some historians, notably Henry Wiencek, concluded that Custis may have embellished his stories but didn't make them up. "It is hard to believe," Wiencek wrote, "that he would tell a lie about a story whose moral is not to tell a lie."

Most historians, however, have found it hard to believe Weems or Custis. Weems, as we will see, told other stories about Washington because of the moral—or perhaps the enjoyment—he hoped his readers would derive from them, rather than because of any evidence. And Custis was never able to figure out how to live a life as someone other than George Washington's step-grandson. He lived amidst Washington's relics, painted murals of Washington in battle, wore Washington's old uniform, and entertained in Washington's tent. Washington loved his step-grandson but was frustrated by his behavior. Just before Custis flunked out of Princeton, Washington wrote to the president of the university: "From his infancy, I have discovered an almost unconquerable disposition to indolence in everything that did not tend to his amusements. . . . I could say nothing to him now, by way of admonition—encouragement—or advice, that has not been repeated over and over again."

Hardly a ringing endorsement of his step-grandson's credibility.

One way to turn Washington from a monument to a man—a way that would have appalled Weems and Custis, not to mention Washington—was to focus on his love life. In 1877, the *New York Herald* published a love letter Washington wrote in September 1758, around the same time he became engaged to Martha Custis, a wealthy widow. What was most appalling was that the letter was not written to Washington's soon-to-be bride but rather to Sally Fairfax, the wife of Washington's good friend and neighbor. The letter was found amidst Fairfax family papers.

"I profess myself a votary [devotee] to love," Washington wrote. "I acknowledge that a Lady is in the case—and I further confess, that this Lady is known to you."

At this point the person reading this letter, whether in 1758 or today, might reasonably ask: Yes, but who is this Lady? Might George merely have been telling his old friend Sally of his love for his fiancée Martha?

The letter continues: "I feel the force of her amiable beauties in the recollection of a thousand tender passages that I could wish to obliterate, till I am bid to revive them—but experience alas! sadly reminds me how impossible this is—and evinces an opinion which I have long entertained, that there is a destiny, which has the sovereign control of our actions—not to be resisted by the strongest efforts of human nature."

If George was talking about his love for Martha, why not say so? There is only one reasonable conclusion: He was speaking of his love for Sally, not Martha. Why not come right out and tell Sally he loved her? Presumably he feared it would embarrass her or, if made public, him. He implies as much: "The world has no business to know the object of my love, declared in this manner to you when I want to conceal it."

The letter was quickly sold at auction to an unnamed buyer and mysteriously disappeared, which understandably raised questions about its authenticity. It resurfaced in 1958 in a Harvard University library, and experts confirmed it was Washington's handwriting. But well before then it had cracked open Washington the stony monument and revealed Washington as a man of passion and indeed lust.

Still, there were many ways to interpret so coded a letter. George might very well have been reminiscing about a long-over fling or just a long-over flirtation. There is no evidence that George was ever unfaithful to Martha, and indeed there is much evidence that the Washingtons had a happy marriage (though details are frustratingly few, since Martha ended up burning most of her letters from George).

The limited documentary evidence of the relationship between George and Sally did not limit some more sensationalist interpretations. An 1889 article in *Harper's New Monthly Magazine* cited an unnamed Fairfax relative as saying that "not even marriage could cure [Sally's] disposition to flirt with the young soldier between whom and herself there had been 'a thousand tender passages.'" Speculation about Washington's romantic life (and not just with Fairfax) was rampant; witness book titles, nonfiction as well as fiction, like *Sally Cary: A Long Hidden Romance of Washington's Life* (1916), *George Washington as Housekeeper with Glimpses of His Domestic Arrangements, Dining, Company, Etc.* (1924), *The Family Life of George Washington* (1926), and *Heart of George Washington* (1932). In this last, according to the jacket copy, Washington's "fierce passion for the lovely woman he could never possess was made to find an outlet in the supreme creation of an empire." Whether Bernie Babcock, the author of *Heart of George Washington*, had read Sigmund Freud is unclear, but Freudian ideas—in particular the belief that great achievements arose from sublimating sexual desires—seem to have very much influenced Babcock and his flap copy.

As Americans rejected the restraints of their Victorian and Puritan pasts, they left very little intact of the dignity Washington had worked so hard to maintain. "Early in life, Washington began to fumble with love," asserted W. E. Woodward in his 1926 biography. "It was really fumbling for he was never at ease in the technique of love and love-making.

"Like the art of swimming, the art of love is one of the simplest within human range, if one understands it," Woodward continued. "Washington, I think, always found it something of a mystery."

Some writers and artists eschewed titillating tales of Washington's relationship with Sally Fairfax and instead portrayed his relationship with God. Weems was among the first and foremost of these. His most famous story along these lines was set at Valley Forge, where in the winter of 1777-78 Washington and his army faced cold, disease, hunger, and despair. Weems told how a man named Isaac Potts was passing through the woods near Washington's headquarters when he heard a voice. "Whom should he behold," Weems wrote, "in a dark natural bower of ancient oaks, but the commander in chief of the American armies on his knees in prayer?" Potts watched as Washington "arose and with a countenance of angel serenity retired to headquarters."

Potts continued home and told his wife what he had seen. "I always thought the sword and the gospel utterly inconsistent, and that no man could be a soldier and a Christian at the same time," he said. "But George Washington has this day convinced me of my mistake." Potts then expressed confidence that God, through Washington, would "work out a great salvation for America."

Weems gave no source for the story, but that didn't slow its spread any more than his dubious sourcing slowed the spread of the cherry tree story. Benson J. Lossing's popular *Pictorial Field-Book of the Revolution*, published in 1852, added to the story Washington's horse tied to a sapling while the general prayed. This detail appealed to many of the artists who illustrated the scene, including Henry Brueckner. The post office used Brueckner's version on a stamp in 1928, and Washington's prayer

The Prayer at Valley Forge, engraved by John C. McRae from the painting by Henry Bruecker. Published by Joseph Laing, 1889.
LIBRARY OF CONGRESS

appeared on another stamp in 1977. In his second inaugural address, Ronald Reagan invoked the image of a general "falling to his knees in the hard snow of Valley Forge," and his listeners surely knew what general he meant.

A *Philadelphia Inquirer* article of 1861 added details that went well beyond Lossing's horse. Here Washington has a vision in which he sees the future of America, including the perils the nation will face. The greatest peril to come, Washington learns, is a civil war—hardly a surprising prophecy for a story that appeared two months after Confederate forces attacked US Army forces at Fort Sumter. An angelic figure assures Washington that America will prevail. "Son of the Republic," the voice addresses Washington, "Let every child of the Republic learn to live for his God, his land, and Union."

The author of the story was Wesley Bradshaw, a pseudonym for Charles W. Alexander, author of various patriotic potboilers. His source, he said, was a ninety-nine-year-old Revolutionary War veteran named Anthony Sherman. Sherman, historian J. G. Bell found, did serve in the Continental Army but not at Valley Forge.

The story of Washington's vision has been reprinted many times, including in US Army newspapers. "And now," Bell wrote, "it's on the internet, so it will never die."

Stories like Weems's and Bradshaw's surely appealed to those who believed America was founded as a Christian nation. They may have been especially popular because the actual religious beliefs of many of the founders and of Washington in particular are hard to determine. Washington served on the vestry of his Anglican and later Episcopal church and attended church throughout his life. He often spoke of "Providence" and "Destiny" as guiding his army and nation. He believed religion and morality were "indispensable supports" to "political prosperity." But he rarely mentioned God or Jesus Christ, never took communion, and was comfortable attending services of other denominations and indeed other religions. As he did so much else, Washington considered his religious beliefs private and he made sure they remained so.

Most visitors to Washington, DC, don't need a statue like Jefferson's or Lincoln's to conjure up an image of Washington.

Those imagining Washington the general most often think of *Washington Crossing the Delaware*. Emanuel Leutze's 1851 painting shows Washington leading his army through the sleet and snow on the way to surprise Hessian mercenaries and British soldiers in New Jersey.

"The image . . . is one of the folk-memories that most Americans share," wrote historian David Hackett Fischer. "We see a great river choked with ice, and a long line of little boats filled with horses, guns, and soldiers. In the foreground is the heroic figure of George Washington."

Leutze began work on the painting in 1848 while living in Germany, where he hoped the work would inspire supporters of the European revolutions of that year. This led the *New York Times* to comment that the painting represented Washington crossing the Rhine and not the Delaware. And the painting is full of historical inaccuracies, among them: The boat and uniforms were wrong for the Continental Army of 1776, horses and artillery were brought over separately, the crossing took place at night despite the daylight in the painting, and the flag in the boat was not adopted until the year after the crossing.

Leutze's work was nonetheless a great success—so much so that Mark Twain complained that by the late nineteenth century copies of the painting embroidered by young ladies could be seen in all the best homes, and that these "would have made Washington hesitate about the crossing, if he could have foreseen what advantage was going to be taken of it."

Leutze's painting also inspired other artists. George Caleb Bingham's 1871 *Washington Crossing the Delaware* moved the scene at least partly into his own century. Bingham placed the figures on a flatboat like those found on the Mississippi River, and he dressed many of those aboard in nineteenth-century frontier attire. Larry Rivers's 1953 *Washington Crossing the Delaware* featured an off-center Washington and an anxious soldier, fit for a period when artists saw heroism as out of fashion. Equally unheroic was Peter Saul's 1975 *Washington Crossing the Delaware*, in which the general is riding his trusty steed right into the river.

Those who want an image of Washington not as general but as president can, of course, merely look in their wallets. The image of Washington on the dollar bill comes from Gilbert Stuart's 1796 painting. The painting was commissioned by Martha Washington and is known as the Athenaeum portrait (after the Boston library that acquired it).

Stuart prided himself at getting his subjects to open up but was stymied by Washington's famous reserve. Though the Athenaeum is the best-known portrait of Washington—indeed, probably the best-known portrait of anyone—Stuart never finished it. The Athenaeum has only Washington's head and shoulders against a partly unfinished background. One theory as to why Stuart never finished it was that he didn't want to turn it over to Martha Washington. Since it was unfinished, Stuart could hold onto it, and this allowed him to make copies, of which he made more than seventy. These provided a major part of his income for years. Indeed, long before the Athenaeum landed on the dollar bill, Stuart referred to the painting as his "hundred-dollar bill."

The Athenaeum portrait appeared on numerous private bank notes throughout the first half of the nineteenth century and, as engraved by Alfred Sealey, on federally issued one-dollar notes starting in 1869. Stuart's portrait was also the source for a 1917 engraving by George F. C. Smillie. In Smillie's version, unlike in Sealey's version or Stuart's original, Washington is facing toward the right. Smillie's version first appeared on the dollar in 1918 and remains there today.

Washington looks uncomfortable in Stuart's portrait and on the dollar bill, and his dislike of sitting for artists was probably only one reason. Another was that in 1796 he had just had a new set of false teeth inserted, and no discussion of myths surrounding Washington ought to close without at least a mention of those teeth: They were *not* made from wood. They may have been made from walrus or elephant ivory. And some of his false teeth may have come, disturbing as it is to hear this about the father of our country, from the mouths of his slaves.

Chapter Six

Betsy Ross's Flag

HAVING FOUND IN GEORGE WASHINGTON A FATHER FOR THE NATION, Americans needed a mother. There was no shortage of female images. Before and especially after 1776, women were often used to personify America. Sometimes they were called Columbia, sometimes Lady Liberty, sometimes just Liberty. But these were all very abstract and monumental, as was the Statue of Liberty conceived by the French sculptor Frédéric-Auguste Bartholdi in 1865. What was needed was an actual woman.

Then, in 1870, Betsy Ross's grandson, William Canby, read a paper to the Historical Society of Pennsylvania in Philadelphia. Canby also recounted the story in a letter to George Henry Preble, who would write a history of the flag. According to Canby, he was eleven years old when his grandmother told him and other family members how she came to create the first flag:

> *Washington was a frequent visitor at my grandmother's house before receiving his command of the army. She embroidered his shirt ruffles, and did many other things for him. He knew her skill with the needle. Col. Ross [Betsy Ross's late husband's uncle, George Ross] with . . . Robt. Morris, and Gen. Washington called upon Mrs. Ross, and told her they were a committee of Congress, and wanted her to make the flag from a drawing, a rough one, which upon her suggestions was redrawn by General Washington in pencil in her back-parlor. . . . I fix the date to be during Washington's visit to Congress from New York*

in June, 1776, when he came, to confer upon the affairs of the army, the flag being no doubt one of those affairs.

The particular suggestion Ross made, Canby explained, was to change Washington's proposed six-pointed stars to ones with five points. Ross, an experienced seamstress, understood the five-pointed stars would be easier to produce. Soon after, Ross produced a sample flag, and more quickly followed.

Canby produced affidavits from other descendants of Ross, as well as from women who worked with her in her upholstery shop. All confirmed the story.

The problem with Canby's story, as Preble quickly pointed out, was that he set it in June 1776, a full year before the Continental Congress passed a resolution that the flag should have thirteen alternating red and white stripes and thirteen white stars in a field of blue. Other than Canby's family recollections, there is no evidence that prior to its resolution of June 1777 Congress discussed, let alone turned to anyone to sew, a national flag. Preble characterized an 1878 pamphlet promulgating the Ross story as "ridiculous."

Other historians were equally dismissive and sometimes quite condescending toward Ross. "The naïve conception," wrote M. M. Quaife, "that at a time when the life of the nation was hanging in the balance, men of the intellectual caliber and heavy responsibilities of George Washington and Robert Morris would fritter away an afternoon in familiar discussion with an indigent seamstress over the trifling detail of how the stars in a flag should be cut and arranged exceeds the reasonable bounds of human credulity."

None of this kept Betsy Ross from becoming the most famous woman of the Revolutionary era.

The man most responsible for that fame was an artist named Charles H. Weisgerber. His 1892 painting, *Birth of Our Nation's Flag*, portrays Ross presenting the flag to Washington and his fellow committee members. The painting was seen by millions at the 1893 World's Columbian Expo-

Thomas & Wylie print based on Charles H. Weisgerber, *Birth of Our Nation's Flag*, 1892.
LIBRARY OF CONGRESS

sition in Chicago, and millions more would see reproductions on stamps and in books, especially books for children.

Weisgerber's efforts to give Ross her due didn't stop with the painting. He was one of the founding members of the Betsy Ross Memorial Association, which bought her house in Philadelphia and turned it into a museum. The museum opened to the public in 1898 and regularly featured reenactments of the famous scene with Washington, Morris, and Colonel Ross. Weisgerber lived in the house and sold souvenirs from there.

Ross's descendants also continued to promote her. In 1899 her grand-nephew, Joseph Boggs Beale, painted the scene for a precursor to movies known as "Magic Lantern" shows. Other early Betsy Ross products included knives, pianos, and—more predictably—sewing machines, pincushions, and flags.

Ross's descendants and Weisgerber had more going for them than their own entrepreneurial energies. Their timing was just right. Ross was an unthreatening heroine whose story came to the fore as some women were threatening to upend traditional gender roles. Canby told his tale just a year after Elizabeth Cady Stanton and Susan B. Anthony founded the National Woman Suffrage Association. Ross, wrote historian Laura Thatcher Ulrich, "challenged George Washington's design for the flag, but she did not challenge a . . . division of labor that put needles in the hands of little girls and guns on the shoulders of their brothers." Even her workplace, which in reality was an upholstery shop from which the widowed Ross ran a business, was moved in Canby's telling to a domestic setting—the parlor of her home.

Ross "became America's founding mother to complement the Founding Fathers," said historian Morris Vogel. "It was the immaculate conception: George Washington comes to visit and the flag literally issues forth from Betsy's lap."

It was not just the threat of women's suffrage that made the timing right for the Ross story. In the second half of the nineteenth century, there was a surge of interest in the flag in general. This had not been the case during the Revolution, when few people paid much attention to the flag's design. Sometimes the stars were in a circle, as Ross's alleged flag is usually pictured, but sometimes they were arranged in rows or a straight line. Sometimes the stars had five points, as Canby claimed Ross designed them, but sometimes they had four or six or eight points. Sometimes the stars were replaced by dots. Sometimes the stripes were red, white, *and* blue.

Interest in the flag increased during the War of 1812, when Francis Scott Key wrote "The Star-Spangled Banner." But it was not until after the Civil War that the flag was widely seen as a symbol of the nation's newfound unity. The Stars and Stripes became even more popular as patriotic feelings swelled around the centennial of the Declaration of Independence. Other flag stories, many as dubious as Canby's, spread around the same time. An 1876 play by Martin Farquhar Tupper has Benjamin Franklin explaining that the flag's design was based on the Washington family coat of arms. That coat of arms did indeed have stars and stripes, but there is no evidence it had anything to do with the Stars and Stripes.

If anyone deserves credit for designing the first flag, it is Francis Hopkinson, a signer of the Declaration of Independence and, in 1777, still a congressman from New Jersey. Three years later, he wrote a letter to the Continental Board of Admiralty noting the government had adopted his design for a flag and charging nine pounds for it. The board declined to pay him on the grounds that he was already receiving a salary from Congress.

By the second half of the twentieth century, the Betsy Ross story was usually not taken too seriously. In a 1954 cartoon, Ross has sewn a flag with stripes and an empty blue field. Bugs Bunny accidentally steps on a rake, knocks himself in the head with the handle, and sees stars—inspiring the seamstress. By the twenty-first century, most of the books that took Ross seriously were for children, and the majority included, either before or after telling her story, a note shedding some doubts on its origins. "While there is no real evidence beyond William Canby's story that Betsy Ross actually made the very first flag," wrote one children's book author in an explanation typical for its hedging, "there is also no real evidence that proves she didn't make it." Another concluded: "Some people believe that Betsy Ross sewed the first American flag, and others believe she did not. It is up to you to . . . decide for yourself which theory you believe." But this author then gave young readers a little push by adding: "Many people have decided that Betsy Ross did not have much reason to make up the story about sewing the first flag."

Perhaps these children's authors were right to give Ross a break. Though she almost certainly did not *design* the first flag, she did produce flags. The records of the Pennsylvania Navy include her 1777 receipt for making ships' flags, then called ensigns, and over the course of her sixty-year career as an upholsterer she probably made hundreds of flags, as well as numerous other cloth products. And though her story spread in part because of an anti-suffragette backlash, it is nonetheless possible to see her as a feminist heroine.

"She is important to our understanding of American history," wrote historian Marla R. Miller, "not because she made any one flag . . . but because she was a young craftswoman who embraced the resistance movement with vigor, celebrated its triumphs, and suffered its consequences."

Miller concluded: "Her story is worth knowing for what it tells us . . . about the working women and men who built early America's cities, furnished its rooms, and clothed its citizens—families who fomented, endured, and remembered the upheaval of the Revolution."

It's perfectly apt, therefore, that in the 1970s sitcom *Maude*, the theme song lists among its character's proto-feminist precursors Lady Godiva and Joan of Arc . . . and then Betsy Ross.

CHAPTER SEVEN

Molly's Pitcher

FOR THOSE LOOKING FOR A HEROINE MORE WILLING THAN BETSY ROSS to challenge traditional gender roles, there was Molly Pitcher.

An early version of her story came in 1860 from George Washington's step-grandson, George Washington Parke Custis, who collected stories about Washington. The setting for this one was Monmouth, New Jersey, in June 1778, at a battle that essentially ended in a draw. Both sides struggled not only against enemy forces but also against oppressive heat and humidity. Custis described how a woman known as "Captain Molly" brought water to artillerymen, including her husband. Then:

> *Her husband received a shot in the head, and fell lifeless under the wheels of the piece. The heroine threw down the pail of water, and crying to her dead consort, "Lie there my darling while I revenge ye," grasped the ramrod the lifeless hand of the poor fellow had just relinquished, sent home the charge, and called the [artillerymen] to prime and fire. . . . Entering the sponge into the smoking muzzle of the cannon, the heroine performed to admiration the duties of the most expert artillerymen . . . The Amazonian fair one kept to her post till night closed the action.*

The next morning, Custis added, "Washington received her graciously . . . and assured her that her services should not be forgotten."

In other versions of the story, the pail of water was replaced by a pitcher, and Captain Molly became Molly Pitcher. The first to call her that was probably Nathaniel Currier in an 1848 illustration. Currier pictured "the heroine of Monmouth" manning the cannon with her dead husband at her feet.

Custis, as discussed in the chapter on his step-grandfather, was not an entirely reliable chronicler. For this story, however, there was an eyewitness, Private Joseph Plumb Martin, who was at Monmouth and whose memoir was published in 1830. Alas, Martin seemed less interested in describing the woman's exploits than in getting to a punch line about her petticoat:

> *A woman whose husband belonged to the artillery and who was then attached to a piece in the engagement, attended with her husband at the piece for the whole time. While in the act of reaching a cartridge and having one of her feet as far before the other as she could step, a cannon shot from the enemy passed directly between her legs without doing any other damage than carrying away all the lower part of her petticoat. Looking at it with apparent unconcern, she observed that it was lucky it did not pass a little higher, for in that case it might have carried away something else, and continued her occupation.*

Since Martin didn't mention the woman's name (or a pitcher), it was up to later chroniclers not only to determine whether the story of Molly Pitcher was true but also to decide who she was.

One candidate was Mary Hays. Her husband John Hays served in the Pennsylvania Artillery. Both John and Mary were present at Monmouth. Mary Hays was a "camp follower"; these were women, often the wives of soldiers, who earned meager wages providing services to the army like cooking, washing, nursing, and, most relevantly, carrying water to soldiers. In 1822 Pennsylvania granted Mary Hays—then Mary Hays McCauley, since she had remarried—an annual pension of forty dollars for her services in the war. The state didn't specify what those services were.

When Hays died in 1832, no obituary mentioned any military heroics. But in 1876, amidst centennial celebrations of the Revolution, Molly

The Women of '76 by Currier and Ives, between 1856 and 1907.
LIBRARY OF CONGRESS

Pitcher's story was often told and portrayed, as in an 1876 lithograph based on Currier's 1848 work.

That same year Wesley Miles, a resident of Hays's hometown of Carlisle, Pennsylvania, wrote to the local paper about Hays's burial, which he recalled was with military honors. Other residents soon dredged up similar recollections, as Carlisle claimed Mary Pitcher as one of its own. In 1903, McCauley's great-great-granddaughter even came forward with what she claimed was Molly Pitcher's pitcher.

In 1905, a local Carlisle historian, John B. Landis, made the case for Hays in *A Short History of Molly Pitcher: The Heroine of the Battle of Monmouth*. The case was by no means airtight. Landis included, for example, a photo of the spring from which Molly Pitcher supposedly carried water to the soldiers in the field. This was later identified as a drainage ditch constructed during the Civil War.

Landis also tried to create a more ladylike image for his heroine. He didn't like the idea that Hays was a camp follower, since those were generally poor women and often thought to be prostitutes (though most were not). So Landis decided Hays, rather than following the army wherever it went, was in Monmouth only because her husband had sent her a letter begging her to visit.

Landis also included verses like this one:

> Oh, Molly, Molly, with eyes so blue,
> Oh, Molly, Molly, here's to you!
> Sweet honor's role will aye be richer,
> To hold the name of Molly Pitcher!

A second candidate for the "real" Molly Pitcher was Margaret Corbin. Her husband was killed at Fort Washington, New York, in November 1776, and she replaced him at his post and was wounded. Her service was more authoritatively documented than that of Mary Hays, since the Continental Congress, in awarding her a pension, noted she was injured in the line of duty. But there's nothing to indicate she was bringing water to anyone and therefore nothing to connect her to the name of Molly Pitcher.

And then there's Deborah Sampson. Sampson, much more than Hays or Corbin, refused to conform to a woman's traditional role. She disguised herself as a man, enlisted as a Robert Shurtliff, and spent seventeen months in the army. Because of her womanly complexion and voice, some of her fellow soldiers called her "Molly," but they never realized she was actually a woman. She was twice wounded but her secret held until an illness led to her being discovered and discharged.

After the war, Sampson recounted her experiences for a book written by a newspaper editor named Herman Mann. Titled *The Female Review, or Memoirs of an American young lady whose life and character are peculiarly distinguished*, it was published in 1797. Mann later arranged a speaking tour for which Sampson appeared in uniform and armed with a musket. Her presentations mixed pride and repentance, the latter perhaps to avoid antagonizing her audience. In Boston, for example, she apologized for having "swerved from the accustomed flowery path of female delicacy." But she could not conceal some resentment that had her actions "been achieved by the rougher hand, more properly assigned to wield the sword in duty and danger," she might have been presented "wreaths of immortal glory and fame."

In general, those who told Sampson's story in the nineteenth and early twentieth century stressed that Sampson, though brave, was not a good role model. Paul Revere, who learned of Sampson's struggle to get a pension, advocated for her by stressing she had changed her unfeminine ways. "When I heard her spoken of as a soldier, I formed the idea of a tall, masculine female . . . and one of the meanest of her sex," Revere wrote. "When I saw and discoursed with her I was agreeably surprised to find a small, effeminate, and conversable woman."

Elizabeth Ellet's 1849 history of women of the Revolution was published just one year after Elizabeth Cady Stanton and other early advocates of women's rights held a convention in Seneca Falls, New York. But Ellet's message was much more conservative. "The career to which her patriotism urged her," Ellet wrote of Sampson, "cannot be commended as an example; but her exemplary conduct after the first step will go far to plead her excuse."

It was not until 2004, by which time women were more fully accepted in the armed forces, that Sampson was the subject of a full scholarly biography. But even though Sampson has gained greater acceptance as a revolutionary heroine, it's still been difficult to tie her story to that of Molly Pitcher. Sampson didn't enlist as Shurtliff until 1782, almost four years after the Battle of Monmouth.

Since the stories of neither Hays nor Corbin nor Sampson fully fit, many historians have concluded the story of Molly Pitcher was pure myth. Others, however, saw Molly Pitcher's story as an amalgamation of many women's stories. Historian Emily J. Teipe compared the term "Molly Pitcher" to that of "G.I. Joe." There was no one Joe, but he was a real type of soldier.

Historian Linda Grant De Pauw has estimated that thousands of women aided the war effort, with perhaps hundreds in men's uniforms like Sampson and many more as camp followers who, like Corbin and perhaps Hays, stood in for their husbands when needed. Historian Ray Raphael noted that when Joseph Plumb Martin told his version of the Molly Pitcher story, he could focus on joking about her petticoat because he did not consider it so extraordinary that a woman would take up arms. Indeed, in Martin's version of the story, Molly was stationed at the gun all along and not because her husband was shot.

"While only two women, Betsy Ross and Molly Pitcher, are enshrined in Revolutionary history," Teipe wrote, "the major contribution of women in winning independence has been blatantly overlooked."

But Molly Pitcher has not been entirely overlooked—or forgotten. Folk songs and ballads continue to tell her story. In 1942, Richard Uhl and Tom Adair released "Jolly Molly Pitcher," whose lyrics urged everyone to pitch in during World War II as Molly Pitcher did during the Revolution. Danny O'Flaherty's 2011 release included as part of its refrain:

> Pitcher, Molly, pitcher
> The soldiers did cry

As Molly ran the water
The musket balls did fly.

Even rappers have taken note. A 2017 song for kids was titled "Molly Pitcher, the Revolutionary Sista."

CHAPTER EIGHT

The Midnight Ride

LIKE BETSY ROSS, PAUL REVERE WAS A TRADESPERSON. UNLIKE ROSS, Revere did not become famous for practicing his trades, which included not only silversmithing but also goldsmithing, currency printing, copperplate engraving, cannon foundering, and dentistry. His fame, of course, came from his "midnight ride" to warn the patriots of Massachusetts that the British were on the march.

Revere himself provided three accounts of the ride. He described how Dr. Joseph Warren, a prominent patriot, sent for him on the evening of April 18, 1775. Warren told Revere British troops were on the march, probably heading to Lexington, where they might capture patriot leaders Samuel Adams and John Hancock, or to Concord, where the patriots had stored arms and ammunition.

"I proceeded immediately, and was put across Charles River," Revere wrote, "and there got a horse." Revere set off from Charlestown around 11:00 p.m. but soon ran into some British officers. He rode "upon a full gallop," and the British gave up pursuit.

Revere arrived at the parsonage where Adams and Hancock were staying. He called out to Sergeant William Munroe, who was guarding the house with other members of the Lexington militia. Munroe recalled the moment fifty years later:

I told him the family had just retired, and had requested that they might not be disturbed by any noise about the house. "Noise!" said he, "You'll have noise enough before long. The regulars are coming out."

Note that Revere did not say, "The British are coming." No witness, including Revere himself, reported him saying what came to be known as his most famous words. This was 1775, more than a year before the Declaration of Independence; most colonists, even those preparing to fight, still thought of themselves as British. Revere most likely referred to the British troops as regulars or redcoats.

Whatever words he used, Revere woke up Hancock and Adams. He then left Lexington and headed toward Concord. He was accompanied by William Dawes, a fellow messenger from Boston who had arrived via a different route, and the two were soon joined by a third patriot, Samuel Prescott. About halfway to Concord, the three ran into another patrol of British officers. Dawes and Prescott escaped, and the latter made it to Concord. Revere was captured.

The officers put a pistol to Revere's chest and ordered him to dismount. They asked what he was doing, and Revere told them he "had alarmed the country all the way up" and "should have 500 men there soon."

Why Revere was so frank to his captors about his mission has been the source of much debate. Some historians have even accused him of betraying the patriot cause. More convincing is the analysis of historian David Hackett Fischer; Fischer argued Revere hoped that by letting the British know trouble awaited them, he would scare them away from Lexington and Concord. Perhaps, too, Revere hoped the British would want to rush this information to their commanders and wouldn't want to be slowed down by a prisoner. Back near Lexington, the British did indeed release Revere.

Revere arrived in Lexington just in time to hear the first shot of the Revolution, what Ralph Waldo Emerson called the "the shot heard round the world" (though Emerson's poem referred to the first shot at the Battle of Concord, which took place a few hours after shots were fired at Lexington). Most of the early reports of the events of April 19 focused not on Revere's ride but on the first shots fired at Lexington. Each side was eager to show that the other started the fighting. Not surprisingly, most patriots later recalled the British firing first and vice-versa. Revere's accounts were of no help to either side: He testified he had heard shots, but he admitted his view of the fighting was blocked by a house.

More generally, Revere's ride did not fit the patriots' preferred version of how the Revolution began. Revere was part of a network of patriot groups that gathered intelligence about British troop movements and passed it on to militiamen via coordinators like Warren and messengers like Revere and Dawes. Such well-organized resistance to British rule did not support what Fischer dubbed the patriots' "myth of injured innocence." In the patriots' early accounts of the battles of Lexington and Concord, therefore, there was no place for Revere.

Revere might also have been ignored because his later contributions to the Revolution were, at best, checkered. In 1779, he commanded artillery in an attack against a British fort in Maine. The attack failed, and Revere was accused of dereliction of duty, cowardice, and insubordination. Revere's superior officer during the battle, Brigadier General Peleg Wadsworth, said that Revere had refused his order to go to the aid of a schooner drifting toward British ships. At a court-martial three years later, Revere testified that he had initially and impulsively refused Wadsworth's order but then agreed to help the schooner. The court acquitted Revere and the court's findings were then approved by Governor John Hancock, who surely remembered how Revere had come to his aid in Lexington.

Gradually the battle over how the Revolution began receded, and Americans came to see the revolutionaries not just as victims of the British but as heroic men of action. This allowed Revere's ride to become a bigger story, especially in New England. On the twentieth anniversary of the battles of Lexington and Concord, a poet named Eb. Stiles paid homage:

> He madly dashed o'er mountain and moor
> Never slackened spur nor rein
> Until with shout he stood by the door
> Of the Church on Concord green.

Stiles was apparently unconcerned that the terrain outside Boston had nothing resembling mountain or moor, or that Revere never actually made it to Concord.

When Revere died in 1818, his obituaries made no mention of the midnight ride. Still, his reputation had improved enough that the *New-England Galaxy* called him "one of the earliest and most indefatigable patriots and soldiers of the Revolution."

What turned Revere and his midnight ride from a regional into a national legend was Henry Wadsworth Longfellow's "The Midnight Ride." Published in 1861 in the *Atlantic* magazine, the poem caught a wave of pre–Civil War patriotic fervor. It began:

> Listen, my children, and you shall hear,
> Of the midnight ride of Paul Revere

Generations of schoolchildren would be forced to memorize the poem, assuring the lasting fame of the ride. Ironically, Henry Wadsworth Longfellow was the grandson of Peleg Wadsworth, the general who questioned Revere's patriotism.

The teachers who assigned the poem to their students were rarely disturbed by the work of the many historians who cataloged the poem's historical inaccuracies: Longfellow's Revere tells a friend that, if British troops march from Boston, he should hang a lantern from the city's North Church tower as a signal: "One, if by land, and two, if by sea;/ And I on the opposite shore will be." In reality, Revere was in Boston arranging for a friend to signal. Nor did Revere row himself across the Charles River, as Longfellow had it. And Revere did not spread "his cry of alarm" to "every Middlesex village and farm"; according to Revere's own accounts, despite Longfellow's claim, he never made it to Concord.

"We have heard of poetic license," wrote historian Charles Hudson in 1868, "but . . . when poets pervert plain matters of history, to give speed to their Pegasus, they should be restrained, as Revere was in his midnight ride." Fischer argued persuasively that Longfellow's inaccuracies were not mere details but part of a systematic effort to downplay the patriots' organized networks and instead create an image of "a solitary hero who acted alone in history"—a loner of the sort Americans have often embraced.

And embrace him they did. In 1884 Webb Miller composed "Paul Revere's Ride." In 1908 Revere's house opened to the public; it is the only seventeenth-century building still standing in the original part of Boston. In 1914 Thomas Edison made the midnight ride the subject of one of the earliest movies on American history. In 1931 Grant Wood painted *The*

"Paul Revere's Ride," composed by Webb Miller, 1884.
LIBRARY OF CONGRESS

Midnight Ride of Paul Revere, his otherworldly Revere was as unrealistic and also as dramatic as Longfellow's.

The midnight ride was further embedded in the American imagination by Esther Forbes's eloquent 1942 biography, *Paul Revere and the World He Lived In*. Forbes's Revere was "destined forever to ride a foaming charger, his face enveloped in the blackness of a famous night . . . to become in time hardly a man at all—only a hurry of hooves in a village street, a voice in the dark, a knock on a door, a disembodied spirit crying the alarm." Children's books about Revere abounded; especially popular was Robert Lawson's 1953 *Mr. Revere and I*, which was narrated by Revere's horse. In a 1963 episode of *The Andy Griffith Show*, Andy convinces a bunch of kids to read their history textbook by telling them a down-home version of the tale in which Revere is "a-hollerin' at the top of his lungs, 'the British is coming, the British is coming.'"

Inevitably, Revere's fame also attracted parodists. In 1896, poet Helen More appropriated the voice of the "wandering, bitter shade" of Revere's fellow messenger, William Dawes:

> 'Tis all very well for the children to hear
> Of the midnight ride of Paul Revere;
> But why should my name be quite forgot,
> Who rode as boldly and well, God wot?
> Why, should I ask? The reason is clear—
> My name was Dawes and his Revere.

An aside: William Dawes's great-great-grandson, Charles G. Dawes, may also have been memorialized in a satirical poem. Charles Dawes was vice president under Calvin Coolidge. He was best known, unfairly, for taking an afternoon nap and thus missing his chance to cast a tie-breaking vote on the president's nominee for attorney general. The poem supposedly began: "Come gather round children and hold your applause for the afternoon ride of Charlie Dawes."

In 1914 the *Boston Globe* celebrated the anniversary of Revere's ride with a poem in which the hero, in a car rather than on a horse, gets a flat tire. In 1926, *Vanity Fair* reported how a salesman for the Juno Acid Bath

Corporation called on Revere's shop but found he was "busy with some sort of local shindig." The determined salesman rented a horse and chased down Revere in Lexington, where he landed an order of three dozen tins. And in 1988 and 1991 a television reporter named Richard Shenkman published two bestsellers debunking myths of American history. The second was titled *I Love Paul Revere, Whether He Rode or Not*. The title was a slightly shortened version of President Warren G. Harding's words on being told, incorrectly, that the midnight ride never happened. What Harding actually said—and it's hard not to sympathize with him—was: "I love the story of Paul Revere, whether he rode or not."

CHAPTER NINE

Poor Richard

WHEN BENJAMIN FRANKLIN WAS SIXTEEN AND APPRENTICED TO HIS brother James, he would hang around the offices of the *New England Courant*, the newspaper James published, and enviously watch some of the contributors praise each other's work. He knew that James, who already thought the young Ben too full of himself, would not consider publishing his work. So Ben disguised his handwriting and slipped under the printing house door a submission from "Silence Dogood," supposedly a middle-aged widow. The opinionated and witty widow announced she had "a natural inclination to observe and reprove the faults of others, at which I have an excellent faculty." The *Courant* published that piece and thirteen other Dogood essays in 1722.

Dogood was the first of many pseudonyms Franklin would use over his lifetime, among them Alice Addertongue, Cecelia Shortface, Anthony Afterwit, and most famously Richard Saunders. Franklin, by then running his own print shop, published Saunders's *Poor Richard's Almanack* annually between 1733 and 1758. The almanacs included a mix of weather predictions, events of the past year, phases of the moon, and times of tides, sunsets, and sunrises, but what readers found irresistible were Poor Richard's down-home maxims like "Early to bed and early to rise, makes a man healthy, wealthy and wise" or "Fish and visitors stink in three days" or "Three may keep a secret if two of them are dead."

Poor Richard, the homespun philosopher, was not just a pseudonym. Like Dogood and the others, he was a character Franklin created and inhabited. No wonder, then, that even in Franklin's own lifetime it became difficult to distinguish between the real Franklin and the myth.

Paul Revere, like Franklin, rose from the ranks of artisans to become a very successful businessman, but it was Franklin who became the archetype of the self-made man. Franklin was frugal and hard-working and not afraid to seize an opportunity when he saw it. "Having emerged from the poverty and obscurity in which I was born and bred," he wrote in his autobiography, "to a state of affluence and some degree of reputation in the world, . . . the . . . means I made use of . . . my posterity may like to know, as they may find some of them . . . fit to be imitated."

Franklin's posterity found him very fit to be imitated. Nathaniel Hawthorne noted that by the middle of the nineteenth century Poor Richard had become "the counselor and household friend of almost every family in America." Students across the new nation were assigned the autobiography, often with excerpts from Poor Richard's maxims that encouraged hard work and appealed to the emerging middle class. Just a sampling: "The sleeping fox catches no poultry." "Diligence is the mother of good luck." "Haste makes waste." "No gains without pains." "God helps them that help themselves."

Mason Weems, the preacher who invented the story of Washington and the cherry tree, was quick to put together anecdotes about Franklin as well. After all, however heroic a figure Washington was, he was very much an aristocrat. Franklin, in contrast, forged a path young people could more reasonably follow, or at least try to follow. "If, like Franklin," Weems urged, "they will but stick to the main chance, i.e. business and education, they will assuredly, like him, overcome at the last."

One nineteenth-century entrepreneur inspired by Franklin was Thomas Mellon, who founded the bank that took his name. Mellon described reading Franklin's autobiography as the turning point in his life. "For so poor and friendless a boy to be able to become a merchant or a professional man had before seemed an impossibility," Mellon wrote in his own autobiography, "but here was Franklin, poorer than myself, who by industry, thrift, and frugality had become . . . elevated to wealth and fame." Poor Richard's maxims, Mellon added, "exactly suited my sentiments."

In the twentieth century and into the twenty-first, Franklin remained a business self-help guru; witness such books as the 1992 *The Ben Franklin Factor: Selling One to One* and the 2000 *Ben Franklin's 12 Rules of Management: The Founding Father of American Business Solves Your Toughest Problems.*

Franklin—and Poor Richard—also had plenty of critics, especially among those who looked down on the materialism of American culture. Hawthorne bemoaned that Franklin's proverbs "are all about getting money or saving it," and "they teach men but a very small portion of their duties." Herman Melville wrote Franklin was a "jack of all trades . . . everything but a poet." Mark Twain recalled having had Franklin's "early to bed" maxim recited to him so often that he took it upon himself to prove Franklin wrong:

> *I know it is not so; because I have got up early . . . many and many a time, and got poorer and poorer for the next half a day, in consequence, instead of richer and richer. And sometimes . . . I have seen the sun rise four times a week up there at Virginia, and so far from my growing healthier on account of it, I got to looking blue, and pulpy, and swelled, like a drowned man . . . And as far as becoming wiser is concerned, you might put all the wisdom I acquired in these experiments in your eye, without obstructing your vision any to speak of.*

Groucho Marx chimed in: "Most wealthy people I know like to sleep late, and will fire the help if they are disturbed before three in the afternoon." More recently, David Brooks called Franklin "our founding yuppie."

These attacks were unfair. Twain and Marx must have appreciated Franklin's humor, and their comments were at least partly tongue-in-cheek. But other critics generally failed to appreciate the extent to which Poor Richard and even the Franklin of his autobiography were characters created by Franklin. The actual Franklin, while perhaps not as spiritual a figure as some would have liked, was interested in much more than money. In 1750, having largely retired from his printing business, he wrote a friend: "I would rather have it said, *He lived usefully*, than, *He died rich*." And usefully he most certainly lived: His inventions included bifocals, a stove that provided more heat and less smoke, and of course the lightning rod. In Philadelphia, he founded a library, a hospital, the city's first firefighting company, and an academy that became the University of Pennsylvania. He had a key role in the drafting of both the Declaration of Independence in 1776 and the Constitution in 1787, and his diplomacy during the American Revolution secured an alliance with France without which independence might not have been won.

By the time Franklin arrived in France in 1776, he was already famous there. He had flown a kite into clouds to demonstrate the connection between lightning and electricity, and—ever-practical—he had provided in *Poor Richard's Almanack* instructions for installing lightning rods. In 1772, he had been elected to the French Royal Academy of Science. French philosophers such as Voltaire and Rousseau saw Franklin not just as a scientist but also as the embodiment of New World know-how, an antidote to the pretensions and prejudices of the French court. Many French aristocrats thought it chic to reject their own privileges and luxuries, at least in theory, and embraced the idea of a rustic republic. For them, Franklin was a proof that America could produce a genius, albeit a backwoods version of one.

This was a strange role in which to cast Franklin, who had rarely ventured into the woods. Franklin was the most urban and cosmopolitan of Americans, having spent most of his life in Boston, Philadelphia, and London. Nonetheless, he reveled in his new role. At Versailles, the most formal of courts, he wore not a robe and a wig but a frock coat and fur cap. "Figure me," he wrote a friend, "very plainly dressed, wearing my thin grey straight hair that peeps out under my only *coiffure*, a fine fur cap; which comes down my forehead almost to my spectacles. Think how this must appear among the powdered heads of Paris."

The powdered heads loved him for it. Women began wearing their wigs in a style that looked like a fur cap. The French bought snuffboxes, rings, clocks, dishes, and handkerchiefs decorated with his image.

To the Genius of Franklin by
Marguerite Gérard (1779) after
Jean-Honoré Fragonard. Open
Access Image from the Davison Art
Center, Wesleyan University.
PHOTO BY R. J. PHIL

They wore medallions with cameos of Franklin. Painters and sculptors demanded he pose for them. Marguerite Gérard's print included as an inscription the words of the French finance minister Anne-Robert-Jacques Turgot. The Latin translates as "He snatched the lightning from the skies and the scepter from tyrants."

Just as Franklin the self-made man had his detractors, so too did Franklin the frontiersman-in-France. John Adams, his fellow diplomat in France, complained that Franklin was so busy charming French society that it was impossible to get him to do any work. Adams wrote in his diary:

> *I found that the business of our commission would never be done,*
> *unless I did it. . . . The life of Dr. Franklin was a scene of continual*
> *dissipation. . . . It was late when he breakfasted, and as soon as break-*
> *fast was over, a crowd of carriages came to his . . . lodgings, with all*
> *sorts of people, some philosophers, academicians, and economists; some*

*of his small tribe of humble friends in the literary way . . . but by far
the greater part were women and children, come to have the honor
to see the great Franklin, and to have the pleasure of telling stories
about his simplicity, his bald head and scattering . . . hairs, among
their acquaintances.*

Franklin's "dissipation" appalled Abigail Adams as much as it did
her husband. She described a dinner where a Madame Helvetius was
"frequently locking her hand into the doctor's . . . then throwing her
arm carelessly upon the doctor's neck." After dinner, Madame Helvetius
"threw herself upon a settee, where she showed more than her feet."

With the coming of the French Revolution, criticism of Franklin's
personal life meshed with criticism of his politics. Members of the
Federalist Party and press, who feared French radicalism would spread
to America, were especially harsh. Franklin was, one wrote, "one of our
first jacobins, the first to lay his head in the lap of French harlotry; and
prostrate the Christianity and honor of his country to the deism and
democracies of Paris." Later, Melville (who had criticized Franklin for
not being a poet) noted that he enjoyed "the homage of the choicest
Parisian literati" and that "at the age of seventy-two he was the caressed
favorite of the highest born beauties of the court."

It seems very unfair to attack Franklin both for going too early to
bed in America and for staying up too late with the beauties of the court
in France. There was some truth to both criticisms, but both were based
on images Franklin created and neither image reflected the full reality.
The criticism from John and Abigail Adams was at least partly a result
of their jealousy and puritanism. Franklin was not above seducing the
ladies of Paris, but much of what the Adamses and others witnessed was
flirting that led nowhere. To Madame Helvetius, for example, Franklin
wrote, describing himself in the third person: "As he has already given her
many of his days, though he has so few left to give, she appears ungrateful
never to have given him a single one of her nights." And to a Madame
Brillon he wrote: "When I was a young man and enjoyed more of the
favors of the fair sex than I do at present, I had no gout. Hence, if the
ladies of Passy had shown more of that Christian charity that I have so

often recommended to you in vain, I should not be suffering from the gout right now."

What Adams failed to grasp and what Franklin fully understood was that the images he cultivated in Paris—both as a sage and as a flirt—gave him access to courtiers who could help the American cause. If the French had had no one to negotiate with other than the grumpy Adams, it's unlikely they would have been as forthcoming with aid to the Continental Army.

In the 1920s, an age or at least an author less judgmental than Adams penned an *Odeography of B. Franklin.* Earl H. Emmons, a printer and sometime poet, saw no need to apologize for his idol's escapades and suggested Franklin could have been pals with Babe Ruth and Mae West.

Is it possible to find the real Franklin underneath what the historian Gordon Wood called his "many masks"? The novelist and critic John Updike saw "many Franklins, one emerging from another like those brightly painted Russian dolls which, ever smaller, disclose yet one more, until a last wooden homunculus, a little smooth nugget like a soul, is reached."

But perhaps that's the wrong way to look at Franklin. He spent so much time wearing masks—and shaping them—that they ought to be considered part of him and not appendages to be stripped away. In the musical *1776*, first performed in 1969, Adams is impatiently trying to round up support for independence in the Continental Congress. He is annoyed that Franklin isn't around to help, all the more so when he finds Franklin calmly sitting for a portrait. Adams demands to know where Franklin was when he needed him.

"Right here, John," Franklin answers, "being preserved for posterity."

CHAPTER TEN

Elbow Room

BENJAMIN FRANKLIN CHARMED THE FRENCH COURT BY DONNING A FUR cap and pretending to be a visitor from the wilderness. But the one who wore the coonskin cap, at least according to the lyrics of the theme song for the television show that took his name, was Daniel Boone.

Actually, Boone preferred beaver to coonskin. Unlike Franklin, Boone did indeed live his life on the frontier. Always searching for "elbow room," he kept moving west—from North Carolina to Kentucky to Missouri. Civilization was always too close behind for Boone.

"I first removed to the woods of Kentucky," Boone told an acquaintance, according to a newspaper report in 1823. "I fought and repelled the savages, and hoped for repose. Game was abundant, and our path was prosperous. But soon I was molested by interlopers from every quarter."

Boone kept heading west, but others always followed. He finally thought he had found a peaceful spot but then, he complained, he discovered another settler nearby. How near? Answered Boone: "Within a hundred miles of me!"

Boone was many things—a militia officer, a surveyor, a land speculator, an elected member of the Virginia legislature. But there is no doubt he was happiest when he was on his own or with just a few others, preferably hunting. And he was an exceptionally skilled hunter, though the stories his contemporaries told sometimes stretch the bounds of credibility.

This one is from John James Audubon, who became famous for painting the birds of America. Audubon ventured into the wilderness in search of birds and found Boone, then seventy-six years old. He watched

Boone "barking off squirrels," which meant hitting the tree right below a squirrel so the bark splintered, hit the squirrel, and knocked it to the ground. Boone stood fifty paces away, Audubon reported, and "procured as many squirrels as we wished."

And this one is from Timothy Flint, who met the young Boone in 1816 and described a "fire hunt." This required two people, one holding a pan full of blazing pine knots and the other holding a rifle. The light from the pan would transfix a deer, which is then easy prey for the rifleman. As Flint told the story, Boone spotted a pair of eyes in the light.

"But the unerring rifle fell," Flint continued, and rather than taking a shot Boone pursued his prey on foot. When he caught up, what he found was not a deer but a "ruddy, flaxen-haired girl." A neighbor introduced Boone to Rebecca Bryan. Boone, not one to be "beaten out of his track," married her.

Boone family members said Flint's story was untrue, and similar stories have appeared about other frontier romances, so this is likely a folktale. So, probably, are various stories about how Boone, whose adventures exploring and hunting could take him away from home for months and even years, returned to find Rebecca had given birth to another man's child. In one version of this story, the father of the child was Boone's younger brother. Daniel, supposedly, was untroubled. "It will be a Boone anyhow," he said, and he told Rebecca to dry her tears. In another version, Rebecca was unapologetic. "You had better have stayed at home and got it yourself," she told Boone.

These stories may not have revealed anything about who fathered the children of Rebecca Boone, but they certainly do suggest the strains the frontier could put on a marriage, especially if the husband—like Daniel Boone—loved to wander.

Boone was most definitely a legend in his own time.

He was fifty years old in 1784, the year the first book about him was published. This was John Filson's *The Discovery, Settlement and present State of Kentucke: And an Essay towards the Topography and Natural History of that important Country: To which is added, An Appendix, Containing*

. . .*The Adventures of Col. Daniel Boon, one of the first Settlers.* . . . The appendix was supposedly in Boone's own words, though the language was clearly that of Filson, a schoolteacher from Pennsylvania, and not the largely unschooled Boone. Much as Boone loved Kentucky, for example, it is difficult to imagine him describing it as "rising from obscurity to shine with splendor, equal to any other of the stars of the American hemisphere."

Still, Filson clearly spent a lot of time with Boone and his descriptions of his hunting and trailblazing largely matched what facts could be checked from other sources. Boone endorsed the book, declaring every word of it to be true. As for Filson, his unfamiliarity with the wilderness ended up costing him his life. In 1788 he wandered away from his fellow explorers near what would one day be Cincinnati and never returned. He was probably killed by Indians.

Even more grandiose than Filson was Daniel Bryan, a relative of Rebecca Boone. Bryan weighed in with a 250-page epic poem titled *The Mountain Muse: Comprising the Adventures of Daniel Boone and the Power of Virtue and Refined Beauty*, published in 1813. In the poem, it is not the love of exploring or hunting that drives Boone west. Rather, as Bryan's Boone explains to Rebecca:

> The sovereign law of Heaven
> Requires, that man should oft the sweets forego
> Of loved Society, Companions, Friends,
> Relations, Children, tender wife and all!
> To tread th' adventurous stage of grand emprise!
> To scatter knowledge through the Heathen wilds,
> And mend the state of Universal Man!

After hearing the poem read, Boone said he regretted he could not sue Bryan for slander. Boone added that such work "ought to be left until the person was put in the ground."

A much more successful poet than Daniel Bryan was Lord Byron, a leading figure in the Romantic movement in Britain. The Romantics glorified nature, so it was not surprising that Byron would find Boone's story appealing, as can be seen in the lines below from his epic *Don Juan*:

> Of the great names which in our faces stare,
> The General Boon, back-woodsman of Kentucky,
> Was happiest amongst mortals anywhere;
> For killing nothing but a bear or buck, he
> Enjoy'd the lonely, vigorous, harmless days
> Of his old age in wilds of deepest daze.

Even as celebrated a poet as Byron could sometimes struggle to find the right phrase; as Boone biographer Meredith Mason Brown quipped, "try yourself to come up with two (printable) rhymes for *Kentucky*."

Back in America, James Fenimore Cooper's "Leatherstocking" novels featured Natty Bumppo, a character inspired by Boone. The first of the novels, *The Pioneers*, appeared in 1823, the same year as Byron's lines about Boone and three years after Boone died. Like Filson's Boone, Cooper's Bumppo is "a philosopher of the wilderness." But Cooper did not become one of the most popular American authors of the nineteenth century by creating characters who did nothing but philosophize. Bumppo was very much a man of action—Indian nicknames for him included "Deerslayer" and "Hawkeye." Boone, too, would not have become an American icon had those who told his story not included lots of action.

A Connecticut printer, John Trumbull, saw the dramatic potential in Filson's work and cleverly edited out the philosophizing. Trumbull's action-packed version of Boone's life was published in 1785 and was a hit both in America and Europe. Daniel McClung's 1832 book portrayed a Boone who pined for the "thrilling excitement of savage warfare." And Timothy Flint, whose 1833 book included the fire hunt in which Boone's prey turned out to be his future wife, did not hesitate to add other adventures as well, without too much regard for fact-checking. His book, Flint admitted, "was made not for use but to sell," and the book was indeed a bestseller. Once, when Flint's Boone is attacked by a bear, he kills it with only a knife. Twice Flint has Boone escape Indians by grabbing a vine and swinging, Tarzan-like, through the forest.

From Timothy Flint, *The First White Man of the West or the Life and Exploits of Col. Daniel Boone . . .* , 1847.

Probably the most famous of Boone's adventures was his rescue of three girls kidnapped by Indians. Boone's own version (via Filson) was succinct: "On the fourteenth of July, 1776, two of Colonel Callaway's daughters, and one of mine, were taken prisoners near the fort. I immediately pursued the Indians, with only eight men, and on the sixteenth overtook them, killed two of the party, and recovered the girls."

Many more details and much more drama came from Theodore Draper, who during the 1840s and 1850s collected more than forty accounts of the rescue, including firsthand accounts from each of the girls, as part of his research for a biography of Boone. Draper never finished his biography, but his papers and unfinished manuscript have been invaluable to Boone scholars. The girls were bored, Draper reported, having been cooped up in the fort at Boonesborough, the settlement Boone had established in Kentucky in 1775. Thirteen-year-old Jemima Boone and Betsy and Frances Callaway, about sixteen and fourteen, took a canoe out into the Kentucky River and a current carried them to the opposite shore, where Shawnee and Cherokee Indians grabbed them. Their shrieks alerted those in the fort. Boone, Draper wrote, "leaped from his bed . . . seized his rifle, and ran to the river with others without stopping even for his moccasins." Boone and the rescue party pursued the Indians for more than thirty-five miles, staying far enough behind that the Indians would not think they were being followed. When Boone and his party finally made their move, he and another rescuer shot and killed two Indians, but a third rescuer missed his man and that Indian "sent his tomahawk flying at the head of Betsy Callaway, which barely missed its aim." Jemima jumped up and joyfully shouted, "That's daddy!" Boone ordered the girls down on the ground to avoid Indian fire. One of the other rescuers nearly killed Betsy, mistaking her for an Indian, but all safely made it back to Boonesborough.

The rescue inspired numerous retellings. Cooper incorporated a version into his 1826 novel, *The Last of the Mohicans*. Artists also were drawn to the story; among the paintings of the kidnapping and rescue are Karl Bodmer's and Jean-Francois Millet's 1852 pair, *The Abduction of the Daughters of Boone and Callaway* and *Deliverance of the Daughters of D. Boone and Callaway*, and Carl Wimar's 1853 *The Abduction of Daniel*

Boone's Daughter by the Indians. Draper's story of the rescue was constrained by the accounts he collected, but others had no such qualms. Most egregious, both for its exaggerations and for its racism, was Horatio Greenough's statue, *The Rescue.* Greenough sculpted an oversized pioneer, dressed in clothes that appear more appropriate for a citizen of the Roman republic than the American one, effortlessly restraining an Indian trying to tomahawk a mother and child. Greenough did not name the rescuer, but the public generally assumed it to be Boone. The statue stood in front of the Capitol in Washington, DC, from 1853 to 1958.

Contrary to so many of the stories about Boone, he did not hate Indians. Boone was captured by the Shawnee in 1778 and spent months living with them. He got along with them so well that their chief, Blackfish, adopted Boone as his own son. Some of Boone's fellow settlers found his relationship with the Indians so unsettling that they accused Boone of conspiring to surrender Boonesborough to the Indians and their British allies. At a court-martial, Boone argued he was only pretending to get along with the Indians to buy time to build up the fort's defenses, and the judges found him not guilty. Still, there was no denying that pioneers like Boone had much in common with Indians: They hunted the same game, they lived off the same land, they traded and made treaties together. Boone heard stories about how he had "killed a host of Indians," but he himself said, "I never killed but three."

But for many Americans killing Indians was seen as part of the nation's manifest destiny, and so it was inevitable that many of Boone's chroniclers would tell stories about (and justify) their hero's battles with Indians. Looking back at his role in settling Kentucky, according to the not-too-reliable Flint, Boone took satisfaction in knowing that "the rich and boundless valleys of the great west ... had been won from the dominion of the savage tribes, and opened as an asylum for the oppressed, the enterprising, and the free of every land." Even works that didn't explicitly involve killing Indians portrayed Boone as leading whites to the West. The most frequently reproduced was George Caleb Bingham's painting from 1851-52, *Daniel Boone Escorting Settlers through the Cumberland Gap.* Bingham pictures Boone as "an American Moses" with Kentucky being the Promised Land. Or as Filson's Boone put it (again in language that seemed more Filson's than Boone's), he was "an instrument ordained to settle the wilderness."

So it went into the twentieth century, when a Boone with nearly superhuman powers found his way into comic strips, radio shows, movies, and television shows. In one episode of NBC's *Daniel Boone*, Boone's daughter Jemima is kidnapped by Indians and a British major. Boone, though injured, tracks them down singlehandedly. "I think we took a long walk for nothing," says one of Boone's friends when they arrive at the rescue scene. "Daniel didn't leave anything for us."

In another episode, after the Shawnee have captured Boone he is brought before their chief.

"I've been told that you were tall as a mountain, mighty as a river in flood," says Blackfish, "that bears, wolves, even panthers run in fear when you approach. I've been told many things."

Answers the ever-modest Boone: "Hard to believe."

CHAPTER ELEVEN

The Indian Guide

"When the white captains wandered hopelessly," a 1926 *Collier's* magazine article wrote of Meriwether Lewis and William Clark, they turned to their Indian guide and "her unerring instinct found a way." This Indian, though just a teenager and carrying around her infant child, "led Lewis and Clark up the wild reaches of the Missouri and over sawtoothed ranges." Without her, the story made clear, the explorers would never have found their way to the Pacific nor made it safely back east.

This remains our view of Sacagawea. In books, paintings, statues, and movies, she is the expedition's guide and savior, the one who led the way west not only for Lewis and Clark but for the generations of American settlers who followed.

The evidence for this view is very slender. Most of what we know about the Lewis and Clark expedition comes from the journals kept by the explorers. Sacagawea joined them in November 1804, along with her husband Toussaint Charbonneau, a French-Canadian fur trader. Sacagawea, a member of the Shoshone people (sometimes called Snake Indians) from the eastern part of what is now Idaho, had been captured five years earlier and enslaved in a raid on her village. She was ultimately sold to Charbonneau. Lewis and Clark hired Charbonneau as an interpreter, and Sacagawea came along.

The journals describe, briefly, the birth of Sacagawea's son in February 1805, her illness in June 1805, the expedition's arrival at her childhood home and her reunion with her family in July and August 1805, and her insistence on seeing the Pacific and a beached whale in January 1806.

They also describe, still briefly, a number of times in which Sacagawea proved useful to the explorers. She foraged for wild artichokes and other food for them in April and May 1805. When a boat carrying papers, books, instruments, medicine, and other supplies overturned on the Missouri River in May 1805, she caught some of the articles that were washed overboard. She acted as an "interpretess," translating various Native American languages, on a number of occasions. Her very presence assured some Indians they encountered that the explorers' intentions were peaceful, since a woman with a child was unlikely to be part of a military operation. And Sacagawea provided some guidance in July and August 1805 when the expedition reached areas she remembered from her childhood and in July 1806 when she recommended to Clark a route through a mountain (now known as Bozeman Pass); at this point Clark noted her "great service to me as a pilot through this country." But she was not in any general sense a guide. Most of the journey was through land about which she knew as little as Lewis and Clark.

"Americans have never had much use for history," historian Richard White wrote, "but we do like anniversaries." White was referring to an exposition marking the four hundredth anniversary of Columbus's arrival, but his words certainly help explain why Lewis and Clark (and Sacagawea) moved into the forefront of Americans' imagination as the centennial of their journey approached. This was an opportunity to celebrate not only the explorers but the nation's successful conquest of the West. Perhaps because Indians were no longer a threat, more Americans were eager to cast some of them in a friendly role. Like Pocahontas, Sacagawea allowed Americans to imagine a gentler manifest destiny, one in which at least some Indians cooperated rather than resisted.

As the twentieth century progressed, new histories and historical novels expanded on the sketchy journal entries and highlighted Sacagawea's role in the expedition.

Eva Emery Dye's 1936 *The Conquest* billed itself as "the true story of Lewis and Clark" but clearly crossed over the line between history and historical fiction. "Madonna of her race," Dye wrote, she "led the way to a new time." The similarities between Sacagawea and Pocahontas increase when the expedition reaches the Shoshone land from which their guide had been abducted. Sacagawea meets the chief and recognizes he is her brother: Like Pocahontas, Dye's Sacagawea "was a princess," and now she had "come home now to her mountain kingdom."

And as was the case with Pocahontas and Captain John Smith, there were stories of a romance between Sacagawea and her captain. Occasionally her love interest was Lewis, as in Donald Culross Peattie's 1942 *Forward the Nation*. Like Dye, Peattie crossed the line from history to historical fiction, though he claimed "there is nothing in the least coincidental about any resemblances to actual facts and persons." For Peattie, Sacagawea's love was "as pure and clear and cold as the sources of Missouri and Columbia" and she and Lewis were "bound by no tie of flesh." But there was no mistaking that what she did, she did "for the love of a man."

More often, the romantic hero was not Lewis but Clark. For this, there was a bit more evidence (though just a bit): Clark sometimes called Sacagawea "Janey" and her son "Pomp," and the nicknames implied he was fond of both. In Della Gould Emmons's 1943 novel, *Sacajawea of the Shoshones*, Sacagawea is grateful to Lewis for his kindness but it is Clark—"Chief Red Head," as she calls him—whom she awaits with "her heart pounding." As was Peattie's Lewis, Emmons's Clark is too chivalrous to take advantage of Sacagawea's adoration, or perhaps he is too racist to consider miscegenation. He does think about it, though. "Of course this little woman was just an Indian, a squaw," he muses, "but was she so different temperamentally from a white girl?" As for Sacagawea, she is pleased both with her destiny and with that of the continent. Her face, Emmons wrote, was "alight with the worship for these white men going to her people, going to send traders to them, going to free them from hunger and fear." The novel was the basis for the 1955 movie, *The Far Horizons*, in which Sacagawea was played by Donna Reed.

Sacagawea and Clark come closer to consummating their love in Anna Lee Waldo's 1978 novel, *Sacajawea*. Still, both see an interracial relationship as impossible. "This feeling had roots between them," Sacagawea thinks, "but the roots could never be nourished and kept alive when the well of feeling had to be kept buried." But at least by 1978

Americans were willing to see Sacagawea as more than an instrument of manifest destiny. She had a will of her own; for example, when her husband told her she could not join other explorers going to see the whale, she went anyway. "She had not come this distance," Clark realized, "to be stopped by a little cold wind and someone suggesting she stay behind and cook." Waldo's heroine ultimately leaves not only the explorer she loved but the husband she hated. The book sold more than a million copies.

Waldo's was not the first Sacagawea to show an independent streak. In fact, among the earliest to turn her into a heroine were suffragists. Susan B. Anthony was among those who used Sacagawea's exploits to make the case for women voting. "This recognition of the assistance rendered by a woman in the discovery of this great section of the country is but the beginning of what is due," she said in 1905 at the unveiling of a Sacagawea statue in Portland, Oregon. "Let men remember the part that women have played [and] give them these rights which belong to every citizen."

As with the romance stories, the story of Sacagawea as a proto-suffragist had some basis, though again a very small one, in the journals. When Lewis and Clark were contemplating where to build their winter camp in November 1805, they put the question to the members of their party and gave a vote to Sacagawea. They also gave a vote to York, Clark's African American slave. The election became the centerpiece of later efforts to paint the Lewis and Clark expedition as an early triumph of abolitionism as well as feminism. The desire for a happy ending may explain why the producers of a musical about Lewis and Clark that opened in Los Angeles in 2003 chose to close their story with that vote.

The musical was part of a new wave of interest in Lewis and Clark that surrounded the bicentennial of the expedition. This being the twenty-first century, there was more appreciation of the diversity of the explorers, and Sacagawea and York were especially celebrated. This still being America, there were also plenty of new products, including cookbooks, playing cards, jigsaw puzzles, action figures, and dolls.

For Sacagawea and York, reality did not provide as happy an ending as the musical: York remained enslaved to Clark and Sacagawea remained married to Charbonneau until her death.

Toy featuring Lewis, York, Sacagawea, Clark, and Lewis's dog Seaman.
PHOTO BY FRANCIS HUTCHINS

Or maybe not.

The standard account of what happened to Sacagawea after the expedition is that she died in 1812. A trader on the Missouri named John Luttig noted in his journal entry for December 20 that Charbonneau's wife had died that evening. Clark may have learned of Sacagawea's death from Luttig; in any case, on a list of expedition members he compiled between 1825 and 1828, he noted that she was dead. But in 1907 historian Grace Raymond Hebard challenged these sources. Hebard collected testimony from Native Americans in three states and concluded that Sacagawea had outlived Charbonneau, married a Comanche man, and died in Wyoming in 1884. To the Shoshone people to whom she eventually returned, she was not known as Sacagawea or any of the other spellings or names previously used; rather, she was Porivo—or Chief.

Charbonneau had two Shoshone wives, Hebard noted, and it could have been the other one who died in 1812. The federal government hired Charles Eastman, a Sioux physician, to interview Native Americans and investigate the mystery. Eastman came to the same conclusion as Hebard. Most historians continue to believe Sacagawea died in 1812, partly because of doubts about the reliability of the oral histories taken by Hebard and Eastman. But others have found satisfying the idea of letting Native Americans tell the story of Sacagawea, or Porivo. Parts of the story they told may be myth, but so, certainly, were many of the stories about her told by whites.

For some Native Americans, one lesson of the Lewis and Clark expedition is that the explorers were successful when they learned from the communities they encountered, and not just from Sacagawea, and that Americans today can still learn from them. "We don't want to be considered the 'Vanishing American' or the invisible American," said Darrell Robes Kipp of the Blackfeet people, one of five Native American educators who collaborated on a Lewis and Clark bicentennial exhibit. "We are Americans; we are part of this country. . . . I think the new approach to Native Americans is not to continue to discuss our problems, but to begin to discuss our solutions, and our involvement and inclusion in everything that goes on in America."

CHAPTER TWELVE

King of the Wild Frontier

NBC's *DANIEL BOONE*, THOUGH POPULAR, WAS NOT NEARLY THE PHE-nomenon that was Disney's *Davy Crockett*, the three-part miniseries that aired on ABC a decade before the Boone show. Within months of the first episode airing in 1954, Crockett-mania grasped America. Stores were quickly filled and emptied of thousands of products: lunchboxes, comics and books, games, toy rifles, and above all fur caps; the price of pelts jumped from twenty-five cents a pound to six dollars. The show's theme song, "The Ballad of Davy Crockett," topped the charts and every kid in America seemed to be singing the lyrics.

Fess Parker played both Boone and Crockett, and Parker's portrayals were similar enough that many a baby boomer never really distinguished between the two. But the stories told about the pre-Disney Davy—and hinted at in the theme song's line about killing a bear when he was three years old—made Boone's pale in comparison.

Newspapers started telling stories about Crockett's eccentricities soon after he ran for office, first for the Tennessee legislature in 1823 and then for Congress in 1825. He was defeated in 1825 but elected to Congress in 1827 and reelected in 1829. Crockett ran as a populist who would defend the rights of western settlers against wealthy land speculators back east. On the campaign trail and then in Congress, Crockett was eminently quotable. When his opponents accused him of adultery, he answered: "I never ran way with any man's wife that wasn't willing." When he was accused of drunkenness, he claimed "whisky can't make me drunk." He bragged he could whip anyone in Congress and also "whip his weight in wild cats." He could also "wade the Mississippi" and "carry a steamboat on his back."

It wasn't always clear if the newspapers printing these stories were making fun of Crockett or if he was making fun of himself. Sometimes he came across as a boasting buffoon, other times he seemed to be getting the best of supposedly sophisticated easterners. Crockett certainly embraced his image as a common man, or perhaps as an uncommon common man. On the campaign trail, he wore a buckskin shirt and told tall tales in a backwoods drawl.

At first Crockett's politics aligned with those of Andrew Jackson, another westerner and another populist, but Crockett broke with Jackson in 1830 over the president's Indian removal policy. Crockett's defense of Native American rights was admirable, but it did not sit well with many of his followers, who were very eager to see Indians removed from lands they wanted to settle. Crockett lost his reelection bid in 1831.

Nonetheless, his fame continued to spread, aided greatly by an 1831 play, *The Lion of the West*, by James Kirke Paulding. The play's main character was named Nimrod Wildfire, not Crockett, and Paulding went so far as to write Crockett to assure him any resemblances were coincidental. But the resemblances were undeniable.

Played by the actor James Hackett, Wildfire came on stage dressed as a frontiersman. Wildfire announces himself this way: "I'm half horse, half alligator, a touch of the airthquake, with a sprinkling of the steamboat!" Similar words had been attributed, rightly or wrongly, to Crockett.

Crockett was not offended. In fact, he attended a performance in 1833 and, to the audience's delight, he and Hackett bowed to each other. *The Lion of the West* was a hit in New York and London.

That same year was published *The Life and Adventures of Colonel David Crockett of West Tennessee*. This book, which drew heavily on Paulding's play and on frontier folklore, featured plenty of anecdotes about Crockett's hunting. One had to do with how he hunted raccoons.

"I discovered a long time ago that a 'coon couldn't stand my grin," Crockett supposedly said. "I could bring one down from the highest tree. I never wasted powder and lead, when I wanted one of the creturs."

The attention helped Crockett regain his seat in Congress in 1833, but he was not as pleased with the book as he was with the play, especially since he wasn't getting any royalties. He decided to write his own book. He may also have been inspired by Benjamin Franklin's autobiography, a copy of which he owned; despite his reputation as semi-literate, he could read and write. He enlisted Thomas Chilton, a fellow congressman, to help him write the book, and *A Narrative of the Life of David Crockett of the State of Tennessee* was published in 1834.

Crockett's versions of his adventures were no more restrained than those of other writers. He recounted how in one hunting season he killed 105 bears, including forty-seven in one month. Sometimes he used a knife instead of his rifle. "I got along easily up to him," Crockett wrote, "and placing my hand on his rump, felt for his shoulder, just behind which I intended to stick him. I made a lounge with my long knife, and fortunately stuck him right through the heart."

That killing took place on a very cold January night, and Crockett couldn't get a good fire going. The way to avoid freezing, he decided, was to exercise. So: "I went to a tree about two feet through, and not a limb on it for thirty feet, and I would climb up it to the limbs, and then lock my arms together around it, and slide down to the bottom again. This would make the insides of my legs and arms feel mighty warm and good. I continued this till daylight in the morning, and how often I clomb up my tree and slid down I don't know, but I reckon at least a hundred times."

Crockett's *Narrative* also described his campaign strategy. He would put on a large buckskin hunting shirt with a couple of pockets, one of which he filled with tobacco and the other with liquor.

"I knowed when I met a man and offered him a dram, he would throw out his quid of tobacco to take one," Crockett explained, "and after he had taken his horn, I would out with my twist and give him another chaw. And in this way . . . I would be sure to leave him in a first-rate good humor."

The book's title page included perhaps Crockett's most famous saying:

> I leave this rule for others when I'm dead,
> Be always sure you're right, then go ahead!

The *Narrative* was a great success, and leaders of the Whig party now saw Crockett as a potential presidential candidate. Like Crockett, the Whigs wanted to get rid of Jackson, and Crockett's western populism could appeal to those who'd voted for Jackson. The Whigs sent Crockett on a book tour, though it was very clearly also an anti-Jackson tour. They even arranged for ghostwriters to quickly pen two more books published under Crockett's name.

Crockett's presidential hopes were dashed when he lost his 1835 congressional race. The tour may have bolstered his national reputation, but it left him open to criticism that he had lost interest in his Tennessee constituents. It didn't help that Crockett had never managed to push through Congress any bill to help poor settlers and squatters hold on to lands coveted by wealthy speculators.

Frustrated by his defeat, Crockett announced his plans. "I told the voters that if they would elect me I would serve them to the best of my ability; but if they did not they might go to hell, and I would go to Texas."

And so he set off for Texas and the Alamo.

Texas was part of Mexico, though by the early 1830s about 75 percent of its population came from the United States, especially southern states. These immigrants were attracted by land that was one-tenth the price of land farther north. The Mexican government saw the influx of Americans—many of them in Texas illegally—as a threat to its authority, and it outlawed new immigration. The more militant Americans responded by declaring Texas an independent nation. Crockett arrived in San Antonio as the Mexican general Santa Anna and his twenty-four hundred troops were marching toward its fort.

Crockett had not come to Texas to fight at the Alamo. Like others, he had been attracted by cheap land, and he probably also hoped Texans might be more willing to elect him to office than had Tennesseans. He was a hunter and not a soldier. But he found himself alongside the other defenders of the Alamo, and his death there did more than anything in his life to secure his legend. In the third episode of Disney's miniseries, Fess Parker is last seen swinging his rifle like a club, with the bodies of the Mexicans he has slain at his feet. In the 1960 movie *The Alamo*, Davy is played by John Wayne and is if anything more heroic; he blows up the fort's powder magazine to make sure a score of Mexicans die with him.

So clear were these images in Americans' minds that Americans were shocked and appalled when historian Dan Kilgore presented evidence in 1978 that Crockett did *not* die at the Alamo. Kilgore was branded an un-American communist. Kilgore cited the narrative of José Enrique de la Peña, an aide to Santa Anna and an eyewitness to Crockett's death. According to de la Peña, Crockett was captured and brought before Santa Anna. Drawing on his famous ability to tell tall tales, he attempted to talk his way out of his situation. He claimed that he'd merely been exploring the country around the Alamo. Santa Anna didn't buy it and ordered Crockett executed.

Even if Crockett surrendered, however, he still faced death heroically. De la Peña's account of the execution told how Crockett and his fellow prisoners "died without complaining and without humiliating themselves before their torturers." And his death, however it happened, focused the attention of the United States on Texas. Money and volunteers poured into the territory. Six weeks after the fall of the fort, Americans, crying "Remember the Alamo," overwhelmed the Mexican forces.

Back east, the publisher of Crockett's *Narrative* and of his two other ghostwritten books, looked for a way to capitalize on Crockett's martyrdom. The death of their author was only a minor obstacle; they were used to hiring ghostwriters. They turned to one to write a "journal" of Crockett's journey to the Alamo, and within months of the Alamo's fall they published *Colonel Crockett's Exploits and Adventures in Texas*. The book contained two actual letters written by Crockett, with the rest drawn from newspaper and other accounts or simply invented. The final entry read: "Pop, pop, pop! Bom, bom, bom! Throughout the day,—No time for memorandums now.—Go ahead! Liberty and independence forever!"

The publisher added a final chapter describing Crockett's death— after being captured. In 1836, evidently, Crockett's heroism did not depend on his dying at the Alamo.

Other publishers also cashed in on Crockett's name and fame with at least forty-five Crockett almanacs appearing between 1835 and 1856, though neither Crockett nor his heirs had anything to do with them. The almanacs were hugely popular. Like Franklin's almanacs, they included some practical information about agriculture and weather. But what readers loved were the tall and often very funny tales, especially those supposedly in Davy's own words.

In one story, Davy explained how he learned about "axletrissity." Unlike Franklin, he didn't need a kite. He was "a leetle in love with a pesky smart gal," but since he was a married man he knew he had to "explunctificate my passions by axeltrissity." So:

> *I went out into the forest one arternoon when thar war a pestiferous thunder gust. I opened my mouth, so that the axletrissity might run down and hit my heart, to cure it of love. I stood so for an hour, and then I seed a thunderbolt a-comin'; and I dodged my mouth right under it, and plump it went into my throat. My eyes! It war as if seven buffaloes war kicking in my bowels. My heart spun round amongst my insides like a grindstone going by steam, but the litening went clean through me, and tore my trowsers off as it come out. I had a sore gizzard for two weeks, and my inwards war so hot that I use to eat raw vitals for a month arterward, and it would be cooked before it got fairly down my throat.*

Added Davy: "I have never felt love since."

In another story, Davy realized the problem with the United States annexing Texas was that the Gulf of Mexico lay between them. "So, in order to remove this one little liquid obstacle out o' the way o' sich a great national wedding, I've jist straddled acrossed the neck o' this pond, like Captain Collossus straddling the Roads, an' commenced drinking it up instanter."

This being Crockett, there were of course numerous stories about his hunting, including this variation on his ability to get a raccoon to come down from a tree just by grinning at it.

> *I war out in the forest one arternoon, and had jist got to a place called the Great Gap, when I seed a rakkoon setting all alone upon a tree. I*

"Col. Crockett's Method of Wading the Mississippi," *Davy Crockett's Almanack of Wild Sports in the West and Life in the Backwoods, 1836.*

... *war jist a going to put a piece of lead between his shoulders, when he lifted one paw, and sez he, "Is your name Crockett?"*

Sez I, "You are rite ... my name is Davy Crockett."

"Then," sez he, "you needn't take no further trouble, for I may as well come down without another word." And the cretur walked rite down from the tree, for he considered himself shot.

I stoops down and pats him on the head, and sez I, "I hope I may be shot myself before I hurt a hair of your head, for I never had sich a compliment in my life."

"Seeing as how you say that," sez he, "I'll jist walk off for the present, not doubting your word a bit, d'ye see, but lest you should kinder happen to change your mind."

The almanacs' writers were almost Shakespearian in their ability to create new words, and their humor influenced Mark Twain. But the almanacs were considerably less funny, certainly to modern ears, when they talked about Indians and Mexicans and blacks. Bragged Crockett in one: "I can walk like an ox, run like a fox, swim like an eel, yell like an Indian, spout like an earthquake, make love like a mad bull, and swallow a nigger whole without choking if you butter his head and pin his ears back." Increasingly, the almanacs reflected the blatant racism of the times. Killing Indians and Mexicans was barely different from killing bears; it was all part of America's manifest destiny.

The almanacs' treatment of women, too, was hardly enlightened, but the writers were at least willing to give them some of the same superpowers they gave Davy. There was, for example, Lotty Ritchers, who "chased a crockodile one evening till his hide come off." There was Judy Coon, who let her toenails grow so that, on finding a nest of wildcats, she "stamped them to death with her feet." There was Sal Fink, who "fought a duel once with a thunderbolt, an' came off without a singe." And there was Davy's bride-to-be, "a gal that . . . I had seed flog two bears, for eatin' up her under petticoat; an' every blow she hit em, war a Cupid's arrow goin' into my gizzard." When Davy courted her (by screaming in the woods), "she . . . climbed up the biggest tree thar; and when she reached the top, she took off her barr skin petticoat, the one she died red with tiger's blood . . . and then she tied it fast to a big limb, and waved it most splendiferous."

A more romantic Davy Crockett emerged in the 1872 play, *Davy Crockett; Or, Be Sure You're Right, Then Go Ahead*. Written by Frank Murdoch and starring Frank Mayo, the play ran until Mayo's death in 1896. This Crockett rescues his love, Eleanor, from an arranged and loveless marriage, and also protects her from a pack of wolves. With a more genteel hero, the play inspired children's books and also at least three movies.

In the 1930s, as Hollywood embraced westerns, Davy-the-lover was supplanted by Davy-the-frontiersman. But no one predicted the

Crockett-mania that followed the release of the Disney miniseries. Even Disney was surprised. The company quickly turned the first three episodes into a movie and rushed into production a fourth and fifth episode, despite Davy having died at the Alamo in the third.

Later Crockett movies couldn't recapture the magic, despite the valiant efforts of John Wayne in 1960 and of Billy Bob Thornton in 2004. Thornton's movie was nonetheless notable for following the revisionist view that Crockett was captured at the Alamo and later executed. But Thornton's Crockett is true to the legend in portraying an always swaggering hero. Brought before Santa Anna with his hands tied behind his back, Davy responds by offering the Mexican general a chance to surrender to *him*.

CHAPTER THIRTEEN

Apple Seeds

HUNTING BEARS, FELLING FORESTS, KILLING INDIANS: THIS WAS HOW the West was won in the tales told about Daniel Boone and Davy Crockett and almost every other frontier hero. But for those Americans who preferred to imagine their march west as a less violent process—and as the dangers of the frontier receded, there were more and more who preferred to see their civilization as, well, more civilized—there was Johnny Appleseed.

His real name was John Chapman, and he really did walk through Pennsylvania and Ohio and Indiana carrying sacks of apple seeds. Starting from Massachusetts around 1796 until his death in 1845, Chapman led the way west, clearing patches of the wilderness and planting tens of thousands of apple trees. The best-known stories about him portray him as eccentric and saintly, someone as likely to give away his seeds and trees as he was to sell them.

"When the settlers began to flock in," reported an agricultural journal the year after he died, "Appleseed was ready for them with his young trees; and it was not his fault if every one of them had not an orchard planted out and growing without delay."

Many of the early stories to appear in print about Chapman were actually not so different than those told about Boone or Crockett. They brought up his apple-spreading ways, to be sure, but they often focused on his strength and endurance: how he walked miles on his bare feet (sometimes on ice), how he could chop down twice as many trees as other men in a day, how he survived for months eating only seeds or berries or nuts, how he escaped from Indians by hiding on the bottom of a marsh and breathing through a reed (and was so relaxed that he fell asleep).

An especially popular story was set during the War of 1812, when British and Indians were threatening Ohio. Chapman, one of the few whites the Indians trusted, was able to pass through hostile territory to warn settlers of an impending attack. An 1871 account in *Harper's New Monthly Magazine* made Chapman sound like a cross between Paul Revere and a biblical prophet:

> *He visited every cabin and delivered this message: "The Spirit of the Lord is upon me, and he hath anointed me to blow the trumpet in the wilderness, and sound an alarm in the forest; for, behold, the tribes of the heathen are round about your doors, and a devouring flame followeth after them."... Refusing all offers of food and denying himself a moment's rest, he traversed the border day and night....*

Despite including stories like this one about his courage, the *Harper's* article did much to transform Appleseed from a traditional western hero into the saintly eccentric his name still conjures up. *Harper's* was certainly not the first to describe him as odd; indeed, an 1862 history of Knox County, Ohio, had called Appleseed "the oddest character in our history," and local newspapers and histories had already told the stories in the *Harper's* article. But *Harper's* pulled together many of the stories circulating about Appleseed's peculiarities, and the magazine's circulation and influence made him a national figure.

Here was *Harper's* on his dress: "Generally, even in the coldest weather, he went barefooted ... at other times he would wear ... a boot on one foot and an old brogan or a moccasin on the other." As a young man, Appleseed wore clothing that pioneers traded for his apple trees, but "in his later years ... he seems to have thought that even this kind of second-hand raiment was too luxurious, as his principal garment was made of a coffee sack, in which he cut holes for his head and arms to pass through...." Most notorious was what he wore on his head: "a tin vessel that served to cook his mush." Such descriptions led a later historian to

From *Harper's New Monthly Magazine*, November 1871.

call Appleseed "a cross between the Scarecrow and the Tin Man in *The Wizard of Oz*."

Like St. Francis of Assisi, Appleseed was famous for loving animals as well as people. Once, while preparing the ground for his apple seeds, he was bitten by a rattlesnake. "Poor fellow, he only just touched me, when I, in the heat of my ungodly passion, put the heel of my scythe in him," he regretfully reported. Another time, again according to the *Harper's* article, "when Johnny, who always camped out in preference to sleeping in a house, had built a fire . . . he noticed that the blaze attracted large numbers of mosquitoes, many of whom flew too near his fire and were burned. He immediately brought water and quenched the fire."

Chapman may not have seen himself as a saint, but he certainly saw himself as something of a prophet. He was a follower of Emanuel Swedenborg, an eighteenth-century Swedish theologian who died a couple of years before Chapman was born. Swedenborg believed it was possible to live in a spiritual as well as a material world, a belief that must have appealed to someone as ascetic as Chapman. The first known written report of Chapman's activities occurred in an 1817 bulletin of the Church of the New Jerusalem, also known as the New Church, which was founded by Swedenborg's followers. The bulletin, which was printed in Manchester, England, told of a missionary who traveled around the West both to sow apple seeds and to pass out books of the New Church. The first known use of the name "John Appleseed" was also related to the church and came in an 1822 letter from a church member.

Most accounts of Appleseed's religiosity tended to play down his connection to Swedenborg and portray him instead as a more generic Christian, albeit a very devout one. The *Harper's* article, for example, recounted how an itinerant preacher—and there were many who roamed the West during what came to be known as the Second Great Awakening—was tediously lecturing the pioneers about their "carnal vanities."

"'Where now is there a man who, like the primitive Christians, is traveling to heaven barefooted and clad in coarse raiment?'" the preacher kept asking.

Finally:

When this interrogation had been repeated beyond all reasonable endurance, Johnny rose from the log on which he had been reclining and advancing to the speaker, he placed one of his bare feet upon the stump which served for a pulpit, and pointing to his coffee-sack garment, he quietly said, "Here's your primitive Christian!" The well-clothed missionary hesitated and stammered and dismissed the congregation.

In one respect, however, Appleseed's saintly image was misleading, for Chapman was actually a successful businessman. He bought many of the parcels of land on which he planted his seeds and ultimately accumulated about twelve hundred acres across three states. He gave away plenty of trees but also sold plenty, including many grown on land he didn't own. And the seeds he sowed cost him nothing; he would gather them in the fall from pulp discarded by cider mills. He wore pauper's clothing by choice and not out of necessity.

Similarly, his choice to grow trees from seeds made business sense. By Chapman's time, many orchardists preferred to graft shoots from one tree onto another. These ensured better tasting and more nutritious apples. Appleseed preferred seeds, according to the traditional tales, since he thought the process of cutting into trees might be painful for the trees. But seeds, Chapman realized, were free and also a lot easier to carry. Moreover, journalist and historian Michael Pollan has argued, Chapman didn't care about the inferior quality of apples on trees grown from seeds, since he knew that the vast majority of his apples were not going to be eaten but instead would be turned into alcoholic cider—the most common drink on the frontier. And for that purpose, Chapman's seed-grown apples worked perfectly well.

"Johnny Appleseed was no Christian saint," Pollan concluded. "He was . . . the American Dionysus"—though Dionysus was the Greek god of winemaking and Chapman's alcohol came from apples instead of grapes.

By the second half of the nineteenth century, hard cider was in decline, and the wholesome image of apples (and Appleseed) could fully take hold. Poets found Appleseed especially appealing.

Lydia Maria Child, who had celebrated Thanksgiving in an 1854 poem, celebrated Appleseed in 1880:

> In cities, some said the old man was crazy
> While others said he was only lazy;
> But he took no notice of gibes and jeers,
> He knew he was working for future years.
> He knew that trees would soon abound
> Where once a tree could not have been found . . .

Vachel Lindsay returned again and again to Appleseed in his poems, writing the first in 1921 and following with others in 1923, 1927, and 1928. Into his old age Lindsay's Appleseed planted his seeds, until "at last the white man hurried past him," until "at last his own trees hurried past him."

Above all others, the wholesome Appleseed appealed to children's writers. In 1933, Rosemary and Stephen Vincent Benét pictured an Appleseed who was elderly and gnarled but sound "as a good apple tree." In 1948, there was a Disney version of Appleseed—how could there not be?—animated and singing and after his death ascending with an angel to heaven where there was apparently a shortage of apple seeds. New versions continued to appear in the twenty-first century; a 2012 children's book concluded with the hope that Appleseed would still inspire kids to change the nation's landscape, "seed by seed, deed by deed."

CHAPTER FOURTEEN

Abner Doubleday's Game

BASEBALL WAS INVENTED BY ABNER DOUBLEDAY SOMETIME BETWEEN 1839 and 1841, according to a letter a mining engineer named Abner Graves wrote to the *Akron Beacon-Journal* in 1905. Graves was clearer about other details than he was about the year: He and some other boys in Cooperstown, New York, were playing the old bat-and-ball game of "town ball." Doubleday "made a plan of improvement . . . calling it 'Base Ball' because it had four bases, three being where the runner could rest free of being put out by keeping his foot on the flat stone base, while next one on his side took the bat." Graves's description of the game differed from the modern game in a number of respects—there were, for example, eleven players on a side—but it was recognizably baseball. In a letter a few months later to the sporting goods manufacturer A. G. Spalding, Graves provided additional details and even included a diagram like one he remembered Doubleday had drawn for the boys in the dirt.

Spalding was delighted to receive Graves's letter. As the publisher of *Spalding's Official Baseball Guide*, the game's most important record book, he had spent years squabbling with his British-born editor, Henry Chadwick. Chadwick believed baseball had evolved from the British game of rounders. Spalding insisted the all-American game must have originated in America.

Baseball, Spalding wrote, "is the exponent of American courage, confidence, combativeness; American dash, discipline, determination." His alliterative energies continued through "American vim, vigor, virility."

A game like rounders or cricket was all very well for Englishmen. "Our British cricketer," Spalding continued, "having finished his day's labor at noon, may don his negligee shirt, his white trousers, his gorgeous hosiery and his canvas shoes, and sally forth to the field of sport, with his sweetheart on one arm and his cricket bat under the other, knowing that he may engage in his national pastime without soiling his linen or neglecting his lady." In sharp contrast, "baseball is war . . . played and applauded in an unconventional, enthusiastic, and American manner."

To establish baseball's American origins once and for all, in 1905 Spalding set up a special commission chaired by one-time National League president A. G. Mills. Graves's letters arrived in time to sway the commission. Mills concluded: "First, that 'Base Ball' had its origin in the United States. Second: That the first scheme for playing it, according to the best evidence obtainable to date, was devised by Abner Doubleday at Cooperstown, N.Y., in 1839."

For those, like Spalding, who wanted an American origin for baseball, Doubleday and Cooperstown were ideal. Doubleday was a military hero: He aimed the cannon for the Union's first shot of the Civil War at Fort Sumter, distinguished himself at Gettysburg, and retired as a major general. Cooperstown was not only the picturesque embodiment of small-town America but also the boyhood home of James Fenimore Cooper, the novelist who turned Daniel Boone into Natty Bumppo. (The town was named after Cooper's father.)

Lest anyone not hear of the commission's findings, Spalding reprinted them in his *Official Guide* and also in his 1911 history of baseball. He mailed autographed copies of the history to prominent figures, including President William Howard Taft and Pope Pius X.

Chadwick treated the commission's conclusions as "a masterly piece of special pleading, which lets my dear old friend Albert [Spalding] escape a bad defeat," and others also found them suspect. Graves was five years old in 1839, making him an unlikely playmate for the twenty-year-old Doubleday. Moreover, Doubleday was at West Point, not Cooperstown, from 1838 to 1842. And on other matters Graves's memory was at best unreliable: Among his questionable claims was that he was a Pony

Express rider in 1852, but the service didn't start until 1860. Moreover, in 1924, the then-ninety-year-old Graves accused his wife of poisoning him, shot her, and was committed to the Colorado State Insane Asylum. There is no evidence that Graves was insane when he wrote his letters about Doubleday in 1905, but these latter happenings sure don't enhance his credibility.

As for Spalding, his bias in favor of an American origin for baseball was entirely out in the open, and he had no qualms about repeating dubious stories. In his history of baseball, for example, he wrote that Abraham Lincoln was in the middle of a game when he was told a group was on its way to tell him he had been nominated for president. "Tell the gentlemen," Lincoln said (according to Spalding), "that . . . they'll have to wait a few minutes till I make another base hit."

Mills, too, seemed very quick to accept Graves's word. This was particularly surprising, since he and Doubleday had been longtime friends and Mills had commanded the veteran military escort at Doubleday's funeral. Yet apparently Doubleday had never mentioned to Mills that he had invented baseball.

Clearly, Doubleday's invention of baseball was every bit as much a fiction as Cooper's Bumppo. Cooperstown's only real connection to the game's history was an 1813 ordinance in which the town's trustees, reflecting a genteel distaste for sports, banned ballplaying in the village center. Because of this, historian Alan Taylor quipped, "Cooperstown can better claim to have tried to prevent the invention of baseball."

It was nonetheless events in Cooperstown that solidified Abner Doubleday's place in the American imagination. In 1934, Alexander Cleland came up with the idea of collecting baseball artifacts and displaying them in a museum in Cooperstown. Cleland worked for Stephen Clark, a wealthy native of Cooperstown. Cleland persuaded Clark to finance the project. He also persuaded baseball executives, including Commissioner Kenesaw Mountain Landis and National League president Ford Frick, that baseball's centennial—with 1839 set as the year Doubleday invented the game—would be a great opportunity to celebrate the game's history.

It was Frick who came up with the idea that the museum could include a hall of fame honoring the game's greatest players.

Also in 1934, Clark found the perfect object to highlight Cooperstown's position as baseball's Eden—a lopsided stuffed ball found in a trunk that had belonged to Abner Graves. Clark bought it for five dollars, and local residents spread a story that the ball had been Doubleday's.

With preparations for baseball's centennial well under way in Cooperstown, a serpent forced its way into baseball's Eden. In 1935, Bruce Cartwright Jr. contacted the editor of a local newspaper with the claim that his grandfather, Alexander Joy Cartwright, was the true inventor of baseball. Alexander Cartwright's claim to fame was not a new one. His supporters had long noted that he had been a member of a group of businessmen and clerks who called themselves the New York Knickerbockers and who played bat-and-ball games first in Manhattan and then across the Hudson River in Hoboken, New Jersey. Cartwright was said to have organized the Knickerbockers into a club and to have written down the rules. Even Spalding had conceded that Cartwright deserved "the honor of having been the first to move in the direction of securing an organization of Base Ball players." In letting Cartwright share some of Doubleday's credit, Spalding must have consoled himself with the thought that at least Cartwright was American.

Bruce Cartwright Jr.'s insistence that his grandfather invented baseball was a potential embarrassment to Cooperstown and to the major leagues, and it threatened to derail plans for the centennial. If the game started in 1845, then 1939 could not be its hundredth anniversary. Bruce Cartwright Jr. was especially appalled by the post office's plans to put Abner Doubleday and not Alexander Joy Cartwright on a commemorative stamp.

In 1938, the organizers of the Hall of Fame found a way to quiet the Cartwright clan. A special committee created to consider nineteenth-century players and pioneers elected Alexander Joy Cartwright to the Hall. How this came about is unclear. There's no record of the committee's vote or even its members. But from that point on Bruce Cartwright's correspondence was friendly and unthreatening. As for the stamp, the

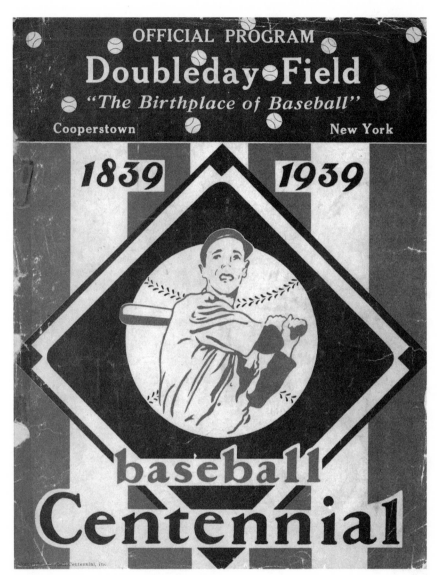

Baseball Centennial Program, June 12, 1939.

THE NATIONAL BASEBALL HALL OF FAME AND MUSEUM

post office helped out by using an image of a sandlot game with an idyllic background of a church, barn, and schoolhouse. Neither Doubleday nor Cartwright appeared on the stamp.

Cooperstown and baseball could now focus on celebrating. The first members of the Hall of Fame were Ty Cobb, Walter Johnson, Christy Mathewson, Babe Ruth, and Honus Wagner, and they were inducted with great fanfare. The official program looked somewhat like the American flag with baseballs instead of stars in a blue field. President Franklin Roosevelt added his stamp of approval to that of the post office, praising Doubleday for his accomplishments in peace as well as war and noting it was "fitting" that the game be immortalized in Cooperstown. The 1939 commemorations proved again the truth of historian Richard White's comment that Americans never had much use for history but did like anniversaries.

Baseball historians continued, of course, to dispute the Doubleday story, and to uncover evidence of earlier versions of baseball-like games and of their gradual evolution into today's game. Cartwright's role as well as Doubleday's turned out to have been exaggerated. John Thorn, baseball's preeminent historian, proved that many of the innovations for which Cartwright had been credited (including writing down the rules and establishing fair and foul territories) predated the Knickerbockers. Even the Hall of Fame now concedes on its website that Doubleday was at West Point in 1839, adding that "the myth has become strong enough that the facts alone do not deter the spirit of Cooperstown."

Why is the myth so strong?

Partly it's because, like Spalding, Americans like the idea that their national game originated in America—even better, in an idyllic small town in America. Partly, too, there's a longing for that single moment of creation. Evolution, whether of humanity or baseball, is a more difficult story to grasp than one about Adam and Eve, or Abner Doubleday and Alexander Cartwright.

"Creation myths," wrote paleontologist (and baseball fan) Stephen Jay Gould, "identify heroes and sacred places, while evolutionary stories provide no palpable, particular thing as a symbol for reverence, worship, or patriotism." Yet, Gould continued, evolutionary stories bring their own satisfaction. Rather than standing behind the mythical Doubleday, we could "revel . . . in a story that may include the sacred ball courts of the Aztecs, and perhaps, for all we know, a group of *Homo erectus* hitting rocks or skulls with a stick or a femur."

CHAPTER FIFTEEN

Ain't I a Woman?

MANY OF THE STORIES THAT MADE SOJOURNER TRUTH INTO AN ICON for both the civil rights and feminist movements were included in *Narrative of Sojourner Truth*, which she published first in 1850 and then again in 1875 and 1884. Truth's narrative differs from others by ex-slaves, since she could neither read nor write. Friends of Truth therefore acted as coauthor and editor: The part published in 1850 was written by Olive Gilbert based on her extensive interviews with Truth, and the later parts were compiled by Frances Titus from a scrapbook Truth collected. If not quite an autobiography, Truth's *Narrative* is sort of an authorized biography, and so a reasonable place to look for the story of Truth's most famous words, "Ain't I a Woman?"

The version of the story that Titus included in the *Narrative* came from Frances Gage, who presided at a women's rights convention held in Akron, Ohio, in 1851. Gage described how many of the women at the convention feared that linking their cause with that of abolitionists would undercut their chances of success. Wrote Gage:

> *The leaders of the movement trembled on seeing a tall, gaunt black woman, in a gray dress and white turban, surmounted by an uncouth sun-bonnet, march deliberately into the church, walk with the air of a queen up the aisle, and take her seat upon the pulpit steps. A buzz of disapprobation was heard all over the house . . .*
>
> *Again and again, timorous and trembling ones came to me and said with earnestness, "Don't let her speak, Mrs. Gage, it will ruin us.*

Every newspaper in the land will have our cause mixed with aboli-
tion and niggers, and we shall be utterly denounced."

Some in the audience, Gates continued, opposed not only rights for African Americans but also equality for women. Truth nonetheless rose to speak.

"Dat man ober dar say dat women needs to be helped into carriages, and lifted ober ditches, and to have de best place every whar," she said (still according to Gage). "Nobody eber help me into carriages, or ober mud puddles, or gives me any best place."

Then, "raising herself to her full height and her voice to a pitch like rolling thunder," Truth asked "and ar'n't I a woman?" She spoke of having plowed and planted better than any man, and repeated, "and ar'n't I a woman?" She spoke of bearing the lashes inflicted on her as a slave as well as any man, and repeated the refrain. And she spoke of having borne thirteen children and seen most of them sold off as slaves, before saying the words a final time.

Truth sat down amid roars of applause. "I have never in my life," reported Gage, "seen anything like the magical influence that subdued the mobbish spirit of the day and turned the jibes and sneers of an excited crowd into notes of respect and admiration."

Truth's phrase—later often changed to "Ain't I a woman"—was embraced by nineteenth-century suffragists and twentieth- and twenty-first-century feminists, especially but by no means exclusively black women. It has appeared on T-shirts and buttons and as the title of bell hooks's 1981 classic work of feminist scholarship.

Despite all this, many historians have argued that Truth never actually said her most famous words.

Those who suspect Truth's words were Gage's invention have pointed out that Gage did not give her account of the 1850 convention until 1863, when it appeared in the *Anti-Slavery Standard*. (It appeared in this newspaper before being included in the *Narrative*.) Newspapers that reported on the convention right after it took place said little about Truth and none mentioned the famous phrase even though, if Gage is to be believed, Truth repeated it four times.

Moreover, a women's rights convention seems an unlikely setting for "timorous and trembling" women or for racists of any gender. The attendees were committed activists and they were meeting in a liberal region of Ohio. The crowd ought not to have been as hostile as Gage described it. Also casting doubt on Gage's story were her quotes from Truth's speech. For example, there's no evidence that Truth had thirteen children. There's also no reason to believe Truth spoke in the stereotypical southern slave dialect Gage gave her. Truth was never enslaved in the South; she was enslaved in rural New York until 1827, when she was emancipated by state law. Her dialect more likely resembled that of the Dutch Huguenots who predominated in the area around New York's Ulster County where Truth—or Isabella, as she was then known—grew up.

Still, some historians have made a case that Truth may have said "Ain't I a woman," or at least something similar. They have pointed out that, even though the Akron convention may not have been attended by timid and racist women, there were certainly plenty of women there who worried their cause might be subordinated to that of the abolitionists in their midst. As for the southern dialect, Gage could have invented that without having invented the famous phrase. And though contemporary newspapers did not report her as saying "Ain't I a woman?" one did quote her as saying "I am a woman's rights" and another reported, "She said she was a woman." These were certainly less memorable phrases than Gage's version, but they made the same point. Finally, as an antislavery activist, Truth could have been aware of (and playing off) a well-known eighteenth-century antislavery slogan, "Am I not a man and a brother?"

Whatever Truth did or did not say at the Akron Women's Convention, her very presence there raised questions with which suffragists would continue to wrestle. Would supporting equal rights for blacks undercut their goal of equal rights for women? Progressive women had no trouble embracing the Thirteenth Amendment, which outlawed slavery. But the Fourteenth Amendment, which granted black *men* the right to vote, was more problematic. Some leading suffragists such as Elizabeth

Cady Stanton and Susan Anthony strongly objected to the amendment, since it prioritized the rights of black men over women. But Truth was already too iconic a figure for Stanton and Anthony to cast out of their movement's history, and when they published a history of the movement they praised "the marvelous wisdom and goodness of this remarkable woman."

And whatever Truth did or did not say at the Akron Women's Convention, there's ample evidence that Truth's speeches could sway a crowd, as Gage reported she did in Akron. This despite her illiteracy.

"You know, children," Truth reportedly said (according to Stanton), "I don't read such small stuff as letters, I read men and nations."

In 1855, Truth approached Harriet Beecher Stowe, the abolitionist author of the novel *Uncle Tom's Cabin*, and asked Stowe for her support publicizing the *Narrative*. Stowe gave her a nice blurb. Eight years later, Stowe drew on that meeting for an article for the *Atlantic Monthly*.

Both Stowe and the magazine had a large following, and the article ensured Truth's lasting fame. (Indeed, it was Stowe's article that prompted Gage to recount her story about Truth at the Akron convention.) Stowe reported what Truth had told her about how she chose her name.

> *My name was Isabella; but when I left the house of bondage, I left everything behind. I wa'n't going to keep nothin' of Egypt on me, an' so I went to the Lord an' asked him to give me a new name. And the Lord gave me Sojourner, because I was to travel up an' down the land, showin' the people their sins, an' bein' a sign unto them. Afterward I told the Lord I wanted another name, 'cause everybody else had two names; and the Lord gave me Truth, because I was to declare the truth to the people.*

Truth was one of many preachers who traveled around the country during the Second Great Awakening, a period during which many chose to interpret the Bible themselves rather than defer to college-trained ministers. Truth traveled through twenty-one states and the District of Columbia.

It was at Boston's Faneuil Hall, according to Stowe, that Truth uttered words almost as famous as "Ain't I a woman." One of the featured speakers there was Frederick Douglass, an escaped slave and a leading advocate both of abolition and woman's suffrage. "Douglass had been describing the wrongs of the black race," Stowe wrote, "and as he proceeded, he grew more and more excited, and finally ended by saying that they had no hope of justice from whites." Douglass concluded the only hope for blacks was to take up arms, and that "it must come to blood." Continued Stowe:

> Sojourner was sitting, tall and dark, on the very front seat, facing the platform; and in the hush of deep feeling, after Douglass sat down, she spoke out in her deep, peculiar voice, heard all over the house, "Frederick, is God dead?"

The effect, Stowe wrote, was "electrical." As in Akron, the tone of the crowd changed immediately and dramatically, in this case away from violence and toward nonviolence, and also away from political action and toward religious faith.

Again, though, there were reasons to doubt the story, or at least the version Stowe wrote for the *Atlantic* and Titus included in the *Narrative*. Stowe reported that Truth had been born in Africa, which was untrue. Stowe reported that Truth had died, which was also untrue (she lived until 1883, twenty years after Stowe's article was first published).

But, unlike for "Ain't I a woman," almost all historians who have studied Truth have concluded she did indeed say something like "Is God dead?" Unlike for the Akron convention, for the encounter with Douglass there was a report written just weeks after the event. According to the *Pennsylvania Freeman*, Douglass had brought the audience to "a high pitch of excitement" when "was heard the voice of Sojourner Truth, who asked, with startling effect, 'Is God gone?'"

Granted, "is God gone" isn't quite the same as "is God dead." Granted, too, the *Freeman* report came not from Boston's Faneuil Hall but from Salem, Ohio. But while Stowe changed the words and location for effect, she did not invent the exchange. Douglass himself confirmed as much in his autobiography.

"Speaking at an anti-slavery convention in Salem, Ohio," he wrote, "I expressed . . . apprehension that slavery could only be destroyed by blood- shed, when I was suddenly and sharply interrupted by my good old friend Sojourner Truth with the question, 'Frederick, is God dead?'" Douglass, perhaps not liking the idea that Truth had won over his crowd, quickly added that once the Civil War began his "quaint old sister . . . became an advocate of the sword."

Truth herself put Stowe's version into proper perspective in July 1863, just a few months after the article was published in the *Atlantic*. Truth told the Boston *Commonwealth* that the article was "not quite cor- rect." She was referring specifically to Stowe having said Truth was born in Africa, but her polite correction could have applied to Stowe's article in general.

The most mythologized of all stories about Truth have to do with her meeting with President Lincoln. The version Titus included in the *Nar- rative* comes from a letter Truth dictated in November 1864 and sent to Rowland Johnson, a white abolitionist. Truth recounted how the month before, she and Lucy Colman, another white abolitionist, had called on the president, who greeted her with much "kindness and cordiality." She expressed her appreciation for his having emancipated the slaves and said he was the best president ever. He answered that several others, especially Washington, were just as good, and would have acted just as he did.

"If the people over the river," Lincoln said, referring to the Confed- erates, "had behaved themselves, I could not have done what I have; but they did not, which gave me the opportunity to do these things." Lincoln then signed a book of hers, addressing it to "Aunty Sojourner Truth."

The *Narrative*'s version of the meeting was clearly intended to glo- rify Lincoln as the Great Emancipator. Other versions of the meeting presented a less flattering view of the president. The original version of Truth's letter (before it was edited by Titus for the *Narrative*) quoted Lincoln as saying the Confederates' misbehavior *compelled* the president to free the slaves; Titus changed the wording to have Lincoln instead seizing the opportunity and thus changed Lincoln's antislavery position from a political one to a moral one. Colman, too, told two versions of the meeting. The first was similar to that in the *Narrative*. But later, in her 1891 memoirs, Colman portrayed an unfriendly Lincoln who made them wait for hours, who called Truth "aunty, as he would his washerwoman," and who when Truth complimented him for his antislavery actions answered, "I wouldn't free the slaves if I could save the Union in any other way—I'm obliged to do it."

The *Narrative*'s version of the story reflected better not only on Lincoln but also on Truth. Titus implied Lincoln held Truth in high esteem. When they were introduced, Truth told Lincoln she had never heard of him before he ran for president. Lincoln smilingly replied (according to Titus): "I had heard of you many times before that." Titus also implied Lincoln assigned Truth to work as a counselor for free slaves. "From the head of the nation," Titus explained, Truth "sought that authority which would enable her to take part in the awful drama which was enacting in this Republic, and that being obtained, she at once entered upon her work."

Later writers used the meeting to further enhance Truth's status. A 1929 article in *American Motorist* claimed it was Truth who taught Lincoln about the horrors of slavery. A 1940 article in *Opportunity*, a magazine that studied the challenges facing African Americans, claimed Lincoln often welcomed Truth to the White House. A 1943 textbook for African American children claimed it was Truth who convinced Lincoln, over the course of many meetings, to enlist free blacks in the Union Army. A 1966 article in *Negro History Bulletin* article described Truth resolutely waiting to see Lincoln and called this "the first sit-in."

By the 1960s, as the reference to a sit-in implied, Truth was lauded as a civil rights pioneer. By the 1970s, she was also established in the pantheon of feminist heroes, though she sometimes seemed like a token African American. Her famous words in Akron and in Salem and her famous meeting in the White House had secured her fame. That her actual words and actions were shrouded in myth might be seen as another way of victimizing an illiterate ex-slave. But Truth was much more in control of her image than that would imply. She first took control of it by choosing the

Sojourner Truth, 1864.
LIBRARY OF CONGRESS

name Truth, then by publishing her *Narrative*. And she sold, alongside her *Narrative*, photos of herself with the caption, "I sell the shadow to support the substance." In the nineteenth century, a photograph was often called a shadow. But Truth must have also understood that an image is as hard to pin down as a shadow, and that she could use that to her advantage. And she certainly understood that the "substance" she was supporting was not just her real self but the causes in which she truly believed.

CHAPTER SIXTEEN

The Log Cabin

TAKE ONE PART SUPERHUMAN FRONTIERSMAN (A LA DAVY CROCKETT), add in a few parts of saint (like Johnny Appleseed), and you've gone at least part of the way toward concocting Abraham Lincoln.

During his lifetime he was most certainly not seen as a saint. To many in the South, Lincoln was a bloodthirsty tyrant. And he had plenty of opponents in the North, too, including both abolitionists who thought he had not moved decisively enough to end slavery and opponents of the war who thought its costs too high.

But his assassination turned Lincoln into a martyr. The moment Lincoln died, Secretary of War Edwin Stanton, standing by his deathbed, pronounced: "Now he belongs to the ages." Preachers across the nation could not help but notice that Lincoln had been shot on Good Friday— April 14, 1865. "Jesus Christ died for the world," declared Reverend C. B. Crane of Hartford. "Abraham Lincoln died for his country." Poets, too, praised him, most famously Walt Whitman, whose 1865 poem celebrated the captain whose "fearful trip is done" but who, as his ship nears its port, lies dead on the deck. In the first full biography of Lincoln, published in 1866, Gilbert Holland chose a different metaphor: Lincoln was "the tree which rose so high . . . and bore such golden fruit, and then fell before the blast because it was so heavy and high." Lincoln was Moses as well as Jesus, "the emancipator of a race," as Holland among many others put it.

Lincoln was so often portrayed as Christ-like that one nineteenth-century critic satirized both the worship of Lincoln and the skepticism about whether Jesus actually lived by arguing that Lincoln never existed.

Pretending to look back from the year 3663, this author concedes that Americans of the nineteenth century and the next few hundred years generally believed in Lincoln, but he says that's irrelevant. "The story of the assassination," he notes, "suggests, in all its details, the hand of a novelist or playwright. The time chosen for the tragedy, a Good Friday night; the place, a crowded theater; the assassin, a professional actor of tragedy; the murderer's dramatic leap upon the stage. . . . The story *looks* artificial and suspicious on its face."

Lincoln's friend and law partner, William Herndon, was also exasperated by the deification of a man he knew to be very human. Herndon interviewed and corresponded with many who knew the youthful Lincoln, but his 1889 biography ended up creating a figure as mythical as Holland's. The stories generally had some basis in fact, but over time they were much exaggerated, sometimes by Herndon's correspondents, sometimes by Herndon, sometimes by those who followed in Herndon's footsteps.

There were, for example, the stories of "Honest Abe." It's credible that the young Lincoln worked two days to pay back a neighbor for a book he'd borrowed that had been damaged when rain leaked through the logs of the Lincoln cabin, and it's even credible the book was Mason Weems's biography of George Washington (as Herndon reported). It's less credible that Lincoln walked miles to return a few pennies he overcharged a customer (as other storytellers insisted).

Then there were the tales of a frontier superhero, a Crockett of the prairie. It's credible that as a strong young man Lincoln split rails in order to fence in acres of land (as Herndon reported). It's less credible he fenced in hundreds of acres at a time (as others told the story).

Herndon's Lincoln loved a good joke and sometimes a not-so-good pun, as did the Lincoln of many others' stories. Once, according to an 1866 article in *Harper's Monthly*, while Lincoln was practicing law in Illinois, another lawyer tore the back of his pants, and some of his fellow lawyers jokingly took up a collection to buy him a new pair. Lincoln's response: "I can contribute nothing to the end in view." This Lincoln was a man of the people because he was—or at least once had been—one of them. "I have always felt that God must love common people," he supposedly said, "or He wouldn't have made so many of them." And he respected the people, having also supposedly said: "You can fool some of the people all of the time, and all of the people some of the time, but you can't fool all of the people all of the time."

Gradually, the Christ-like figure and the western folk hero blended into a single Lincoln. This process was much advanced by Carl Sandburg, a poet whose six-volume biography of Lincoln firmly established him as an ordinary man, albeit one who is extraordinarily wise and witty and strong. Born in a log cabin, Lincoln rises from obscurity to save democracy. Sandburg set the tone for a spate of movies, novels, kids' books, and television shows that found in Lincoln whatever their creators thought best in America.

By the 1930s, Lincoln appealed to virtually everyone. Both Republicans and Democrats claimed to have inherited Lincoln's mantle. Henry Fonda found Lincoln so intimidatingly iconic that he originally turned down the chance to play him. Director John Ford convinced Fonda to star in the 1939 movie, *Young Mr. Lincoln,* by stressing the movie was not about the Great Emancipator but about the pre-presidential Lincoln. But Fonda's young Lincoln is still heroic: As a lawyer, he defends a man wrongly accused of murder. First, he saves him from a lynching. Then, in the courtroom, he proves the prosecution's star witness was actually the murderer.

Even in the twenty-first century, Lincoln continued to be almost everyone's hero: In the 2009 play, *Abraham Lincoln's Big, Gay Dance Party,* he champions gay rights. In a 2010 Geico ad for car insurance, Honest Abe is unable to lie when his wife asks, "Does this dress make my backside look big?" In the 2012 movie, *Abraham Lincoln: Vampire Hunter,* he takes on Confederate undead. That same year, Steven Spielberg's *Lincoln* starred Daniel Day-Lewis even though Lewis, like Fonda, initially hesitated to take the role. "I never, ever felt that depth of love for another human being that I never met," said Lewis. "And that's, I think, probably the effect that Lincoln has on most people that take the time to discover him."

What turned the joking frontiersman into the nation's savior? According to Herndon, it was the loss of his one true love.

This was Ann Rutledge, "the most attractive young lady whom up to that time he had ever met." Lincoln eventually proposed and she accepted, but they agreed to put off the wedding until he had completed his law studies. Alas, she caught a fever and died in August 1835. Lincoln despaired. Speaking about her grave, he told one of Herndon's correspondents: "My heart lies buried there." But, Herndon wrote, with his love "rudely torn from him," he turned to "the great world, throbbing with life but cold and heartless."

Historians continue to debate what if any sort of romance really took place between Abe and Ann, but storytellers couldn't resist embellishments. Sandburg was characteristically poetic: "He was twenty-six, she was twenty-two; the earth was their footstool; the sky was a sheaf of blue dreams; the rise of the blood-gold rim of a full moon in the evening was almost too much to live, see, and remember." After she died, he was bereft. Slowly, he recovered, except "it was said that the shadows of a burning he had been through were fixed in the depths of his eyes, and he was a changed man keeping to himself the gray mystery of the change."

In *Young Mr. Lincoln*, Fonda kneels by his love's grave, deciding whether he ought to listen to what he knows she would tell him to do: "Go on Abe, make something of yourself."

In stark contrast to Ann Rutledge, the woman Lincoln actually married, Mary Todd, traditionally has been portrayed as extraordinarily unpleasant. Herndon, who knew her personally, described her as snobbish, spoiled, argumentative, and ill-tempered. Lincoln had so many doubts about marrying her that in 1841 he left her at the altar; the next year, "to save his honor," he married her, even though he didn't love her. The result was "years of self-torture, sacrificial pangs, and the loss forever of a happy home."

If Ann Rutledge inspired Lincoln to turn to the world, Mary Todd did the same—if only so he could get out of the house. Mary Todd pushed him to succeed but only to satisfy her own ambitions. "In him she saw," Herndon wrote, "position in society, prominence in the world, and the grandest social distinction."

Mary Todd was the villain of many stories about Lincoln. Sometimes she was portrayed as violent, chasing Lincoln with a stick or a knife. This only added to Lincoln's luster: Even before John Wilkes Booth assassinated Lincoln, his wife had made him into a martyr.

Some historians have come to Mary Todd's defense. A few have questioned whether Lincoln actually left her at the altar. They have noted that there's no contemporary account of this and that the couple may have jointly decided to break up. More fundamentally, Todd was politically and socially savvy and provided useful advice during his campaigns and presidency. And in further defense of Todd, it must have been difficult to live with Lincoln, who was often depressed. Todd stood by him through not only a Civil War but also the death of two children. She, too, was depressed, and in 1875 her mental illnesses led to her being committed to a private asylum.

Some additional sympathy for Todd grew out of an argument put forward by psychologist C. A. Tripp, whose 2004 book claimed Lincoln was gay. Tripp gathered stories of Lincoln sharing beds with various men, but most historians thought the evidence at best circumstantial. His relationships with these men were warm but not sexual. His relationship with his wife was not ideal, but that was not because Lincoln preferred men.

Lincoln's deification required some contortions, especially on the part of southerners. For him to be generally accepted as the nation's savior, they, too, had to embrace him. This took time and there were certainly holdouts. Well into the twentieth century, organizations like the United Daughters of the Confederacy continued to demonize Lincoln as a dictator out to destroy southern civilization.

Gradually, though, southerners accepted Lincoln as one of their own. The story they told went like this: It was not Lincoln but the Radical Republicans in Congress who had been the enemies of the Confederacy. Had Lincoln lived, the nation would have been spared the horrors of the Reconstruction era, when vindictive Negroes and northerners seized control of the South.

This Lincoln—one who loved the South and who could in turn be loved by southerners—was captured in Mary Raymond Shipman Andrews's short story "The Perfect Tribute," which was first published in *Scribner's Magazine* in 1906 and later became a book read in schools across the nation. Andrews described how Lincoln wrote his Gettysburg Address on some scraps of paper while on the train en route to give the speech. When he delivers the address honoring the dead soldiers of both North and South he is greeted by silence, and he takes this to mean his words were a failure. Back in Washington, Lincoln runs into a boy of fifteen whose brother, a Confederate soldier, is dying in a prison hospital and needs a lawyer to prepare his will. Lincoln tells the boy, who has no idea he is speaking to the president, that he has practiced some law, and together they go to the brother's bedside. There the Confederate soldier, who also does not know who he's talking to, tells him how moved he was by Lincoln's speech, which he has read in the newspaper and now reads aloud in the hospital. Again the speech is met with silence, but this time the soldier breaks it to say: "It is only the greatest who can be a partisan without bitterness, and only such today may call himself not Northern or Southern, but American." The soldier then asks the lawyer whether he agrees, and Lincoln answers: "I believe it is a good speech."

Many southerners came to see Lincoln as having fought not only for the Union but also for the white race. Lincoln was a hero in overtly racist works like Thomas Dixon's 1905 novel *The Clansman*, which in 1915 became D. W. Griffith's movie *The Birth of a Nation*. Book and movie celebrated Lincoln—and the Ku Klux Klan. Arguing with a Radical Republican, this Lincoln pushes for all blacks to be expelled from America. Says Dixon's Lincoln: "We can never attain the ideal Union our fathers dreamed, with millions of an alien, inferior race among us, whose assimilation is neither possible nor desirable."

Northerners, too, came to accept the view that Reconstruction was a disaster and that Lincoln, if he'd lived, would have averted it. Sandburg expressed the national consensus in 1939 in the final volume of his biography. "Lincoln had his choice of going with those who, to win a complete and abstract justice for the Negro, would not hesitate about making the South a vast graveyard of slaughtered whites, with Negro State governments established and upheld by Northern white bayonets," he wrote. "From this . . . Lincoln receded," he continued, "preferring 'malice toward none,' 'charity for all.'"

The image of Lincoln holding back the radicals of his own party culminated in a theory that the mastermind behind his assassination was Lincoln's own secretary of war, the Radical Republican Edwin Stanton. This conspiracy theory was set forth in a 1937 book by Otto Eisenschiml, a chemist and businessman. Stanton, Eisenschiml argued, feared Lincoln would be too soft on the South. So he recruited John Wilkes Booth to kill the president. Then he made sure Booth was shot and the other conspirators hanged so no one could talk. In the realm of Lincoln mythology, Stanton's villainy far surpassed that of the hapless Mary Todd.

Believers in this conspiracy theory also tended to believe in the innocence of Samuel Mudd, a Maryland doctor who treated Booth hours after he shot Lincoln and who was found guilty of helping Booth plan the assassination and then helping him to escape. Mudd's supporters claimed the doctor was merely obeying his Hippocratic Oath and treating a sick man. President Andrew Johnson pardoned Mudd in 1869, and Presidents Jimmy Carter and Ronald Reagan both concluded Mudd was unfairly convicted. But the evidence against Mudd is damning: Mudd had met with Booth three times before Booth arrived at his house needing medical aid. In fact, Mudd and Booth had been introduced to each other by a known Confederate agent.

Conspiracy theories implicating Stanton continue to be popular. Bill O'Reilly, then a Fox News host, gave them new life in his 2016 book on the assassination, though O'Reilly and his coauthor Martin Dugard conceded the evidence against Stanton is circumstantial. The evidence is actually less than circumstantial; it's flimsy. Booth was nobody's puppet. He and his co-conspirators, including Mudd, were ardent Confederates. The assassination took place just five days after Robert E. Lee surrendered at Appomattox. By killing Lincoln, they hoped to avenge Lee's defeat and to throw the Union into chaos.

The conspiracy theories, like all the stories that appealed to Confederate sympathizers, depended on a view of Lincoln as sympathetic to their cause. Was this truly the case? Was the Great Emancipator actually a racist?

The southerners who saw Lincoln as one of them could point to various Lincoln words and deeds. Before the war, Lincoln had advocated compensating slaveowners for their losses and deporting the freed men and women. When the war began, he stressed its purpose was to preserve the Union and not to end slavery. Lincoln did not issue his Emancipation Proclamation until 1863, nearly two years into the war, and even then its provisions freed only a fraction of those enslaved. His condemnations of slavery stopped well short of endorsing equal rights for formerly enslaved people.

Historians continue to debate whether Lincoln was a racist or a pragmatist who saw the limits of what could be accomplished in the mid-nineteenth century and pushed for what was possible. It is well beyond the scope of this book to resolve these issues. But this much is clear: Lincoln's attitudes on race evolved over time. And many historians have convincingly argued that—contrary to the neo-Confederates' belief—he was moving toward and not away from the Radical Republican positions. Lincoln was not an abolitionist when he entered politics, but he became one. Lincoln was not a believer in equal rights when he died, but had he lived perhaps he would have become one.

There's little doubt that Lincoln hated slavery. It was, he said in an 1858 speech, a "vast moral evil." In an 1864 letter, he wrote: "If slavery is not wrong, nothing is wrong. I cannot remember when I did not so think, and feel." Yet in that same letter he quickly added: "I have never understood that the Presidency conferred an unrestricted right to act officially upon this judgment and feeling."

Given Lincoln's ambivalence about abolitionism and about equal rights, it's not surprising that some African Americans felt ambivalent about Lincoln. "Viewed from the genuine abolition ground," the formerly enslaved Frederick Douglass wrote in 1892, "Mr. Lincoln seemed tardy, cold, dull, and indifferent; but measuring him by the sentiment of his country, a sentiment he was bound as a statesman to consult, he was swift, zealous, radical, and determined." Douglass also believed that, though Lincoln loathed slavery, he "shared the prejudices of his white fellow-countrymen against the negro." Witness, too, the conflicting accounts of Lincoln's meeting with the formerly enslaved Sojourner

Truth; by some accounts he was warm and welcoming and by others cold and curt.

As the civil rights movement gained momentum during the 1950s and 1960s, many African Americans joined Douglass in backing away from their earlier adulation of the Great Emancipator. They resented the compromises Lincoln had made with slaveowners. They also resented the implication that they had nothing to do with their own emancipation and had depended entirely on the deliverance of some great white father.

In a 1964 interview, Malcolm X expressed his disgust with Lincoln: "He was interested in saving the Union. Well, most Negroes have been tricked into thinking Lincoln was a Negro lover whose primary aim was to free them, and he died because he freed them. I think Lincoln did more to deceive Negroes and to make the race problem in this country worse than any man in history."

It was not just blacks who were retreating from their hero worship. By the 1960s and 1970s, many Americans, especially on the left, were questioning whether American history was as glorious as they'd been taught, and whether American heroes were as heroic as they'd thought. By the late twentieth century and continuing to the present, students have been introduced to a more multicultural history that has fostered a greater understanding of what that history meant for others besides white men, especially Native Americans and African Americans. As a result, figures like Washington and Lincoln no longer tower over the American landscape as much as they once did.

In February 1988, the *New Yorker* magazine cover was an illustration of Washington and Lincoln exchanging Valentine's Day cards, the point being that Valentine's Day had surpassed either's birthday as the most important holiday of the month. Most Americans no longer celebrate either Washington's or Lincoln's birthday, with Presidents Day being primarily an opportunity for a three-day weekend.

Even the log cabin, long a symbol of how Lincoln (and any American) could rise from humble origins to become president of the United States, turns out to have a more complicated history than most thought. Millions of Americans visited the cabin at Sinking Springs Farm in Hodgenville, Kentucky, and came away thinking they'd seen the cabin

Undated postcard, created by Kramer Art Co., Cincinnati, Ohio. The card's caption reads: "Birth Place of Abraham Lincoln."
LIBRARY OF CONGRESS

where Lincoln was born. Historians had long questioned whether this was the case, and in 2004 a dendrochronologist examined logs from the cabin and determined the oldest one dated to 1848—almost forty years after Lincoln was born. The National Park Service, which administers the site, now describes it as the "symbolic birth cabin."

As with so many stories about Lincoln, however, the site ought not to be reduced to nothing but a hoax: Lincoln was born in a log cabin, albeit a different one, and that cabin did once stand on Sinking Springs Farm.

CHAPTER SEVENTEEN

The Lost Cause

THE SOUTH HAD SURRENDERED, CONCEDED THE VIRGINIAN JOURNALIST Edward Pollard in his 1866 book, *The Lost Cause: A New Southern History of the War of the Confederates.* But, Pollard stressed, what the war had decided was that the Union would continue. "The war did not decide negro equality," Pollard wrote, "it did not decide negro suffrage; it did not decide state rights, . . . it did not decide the right of a people . . . to maintain self-respect in the face of adversity. And these things which the war did not decide, the Southern people will still cling to, still claim, and still assert."

And assert they did.

White southerners, including many ex-Confederates, reclaimed some control over state governments as early as the fall of 1865. Over the next two decades, they instituted a variety of measures such as literacy tests and poll taxes that prevented ex-slaves from voting. Jim Crow laws and Ku Klux Klan vigilantism further secured white supremacy. In 1877, when the last Union troops were pulled from the South, the issue of equal rights was essentially gone from the national agenda.

Pollard also set forth other elements of what would become the Lost Cause creed: Slavery, as practiced in the South, was not the odious system portrayed by northern propaganda; rather, it had "elevated the African" and "made him altogether the most striking type in the world of cheerfulness and contentment." And in any case, the war had not been about slavery but about the South's effort to preserve its "refined and sentimental" civilization against the incursions of the "coarse and materialistic" North.

It was not so surprising that many southerners should choose to look back on a largely mythical path when chivalrous gentlemen protected glamorous belles amidst happy and loyal servants. Nor was it so surprising they would choose to see the war as about something other than slavery; despite defenses of slavery like Pollard's, most southerners had trouble portraying slavery as a noble cause. What was surprising was the extent to which northerners bought into all this. Generations of schoolchildren, in the North as well as the South, were taught that the Civil War was fought not over slavery but over "states' rights."

How did the losers of the war come to define its history? How did northerners come to accept the southern view of the war?

Ironically, it was those who fought the war—and who you might think would therefore hold a grudge against their enemies—who first brought North and South together. Veterans on both sides could agree that all had fought nobly, and that those who died deserved to be honored. In the years that followed the war, Americans honored the dead in spring on what was called "Decoration Day"—because graves were decorated with flowers and other memorials—and later came to be known as Memorial Day. Speakers from both North and South spoke of heroic battles and deeds. Northerners could glory in their victories, while southerners could stress how they persisted despite the superior manpower and arms of the North.

As early as 1867, the *Atlantic Monthly* published a poem honoring the dead of both the North and South:

> Under the sod and the dew,
>   Waiting the judgment day;—
> Under the roses, the Blue,
>   Under the lilies, the Gray.

By the 1870s, veterans of North and South frequently got together on Decoration Days. In the 1880s, the *Century Magazine* published a series of articles titled "Battles and Leaders of the Civil War," with entries by authors from both sides. "No time could be fitter," the magazine's editors wrote in introducing the series, "for a publication of this kind than the present, when the passions and prejudices of the Civil War have nearly faded out of our politics, and its heroic events are passing into our common history where motives will be weighed without malice, and valor praised without distinction of uniform."

Southern generals came in for special praise. Stonewall Jackson's death in 1863, when he was accidentally shot by his own men, turned him into a martyr. Jackson was such a brilliant tactician, as the *Century Magazine* and others told it, that had he lived the Confederacy might have won. But the foremost hero of the Lost Cause was unquestionably Robert E. Lee. Outnumbered and outarmed, Lee had kept the cause alive as long as humanly possible. At Appomattox, recalled Confederate general Jubal Early in 1872, Lee "had not been conquered in battle, but surrendered because he no longer had an army with which to give battle. What he surrendered was the mere skeleton, the mere ghost of the Army of Northern Virginia, which had been gradually worn down by the combined agencies of numbers, steam-power, railroads, mechanism, and all the resources of physical science."

Even Lee's crucial defeat at Gettysburg wasn't his fault, according to his many admirers. Lee had only lost at Gettysburg because General James Longstreet was too slow to follow his orders. For southerners, Longstreet was the perfect scapegoat, since he was one of the few southern generals who after the war became a Republican—the party of Lincoln!—and even accepted a federal job under President Ulysses Grant. If Longstreet betrayed the cause after the war, many southerners decided, he must have done so during it as well.

Monuments to southern heroes offered a chance not to mourn but to celebrate the Lost Cause. In Richmond, Virginia, fifty thousand people gathered for the 1876 unveiling of a statue of Stonewall Jackson. In 1890, the unveiling of Robert E. Lee's statue there drew between one hundred thousand and one hundred fifty thousand. The *New York Times's* front-page story quoted at length the speech of Confederate colonel Archer Anderson, who told the crowd that "in every part of America, the character and fame of Robert Edward Lee are treasured." By then, Lee was indeed a northern as well as a southern treasure. In part, this was because after the war Lee had consistently urged reconciliation between the former enemies, but it was more than that; northerners embraced Lee because northerners had largely come to agree with the southerner's view of the war.

Richmond's Monument Avenue added Jefferson Davis, the president of the Confederacy, in 1907. Since Davis had not been a soldier, it was difficult to see his monument as anything other than a vindication of the southern cause, and local newspapers trumpeted it as such.

Monuments to Confederate soldiers were erected in towns large and small throughout the South. Richmond's monuments were dwarfed by those cut into Georgia's Stone Mountain. Begun in 1923 and finally completed in 1972, the carvings portrayed Jackson, Lee, and Davis on horseback and are larger than those of the presidents on Mount Rushmore.

Many of the monuments were the work of local organizations, but larger organizations ultimately took as their mission raising money for monuments and, more generally, spreading the word about the Confederate cause. The Southern Historical Society was founded in 1869, the United Confederate Veterans in 1889, and the United Daughters of the Confederacy in 1894. Again and again, their publications hammered home the message: The war was not about slavery. Besides, slaves had been happy. And besides that, northern traders had forced slavery upon the South. Many of these organizations objected to the term "Civil War," preferring "War Between the States" or "Lincoln's War" or best of all "War of Northern Aggression."

The United Confederate Veterans and the United Daughters of the Confederacy were especially aggressive in pushing their view of the war in schools. In 1897, the former's magazine spelled out its goal: "It is not expected that Southern teachers will instruct the children that their fathers were traitors and rebels," the *Confederate Veteran* proclaimed, "and it would be a curse to the nation if they did. The Southern people desire to retain . . . the knowledge that their conduct was honorable throughout, and that their submission at last to overwhelming numbers and resources

Robert E. Lee Monument, Richmond, Virginia, photographed between 1905 and 1915, Detroit Publishing Company.
LIBRARY OF CONGRESS

in no way blackened their motives or established the wrong of the cause for which they fought."

The South for which they fought never really existed, but writers and moviemakers brought it alive.

The Virginian Thomas Nelson Page wrote of gallant knights and black servants, often using the latter as his narrators. In Page's "Marse Chan: A Tale of Old Virginia," Sam reminisces about the days of slavery: "Dem wuz good ole times, marster,—de bes' Sam ever see!" In another of Page's stories, "Meh Lady," an old ex-slave recounts a romance between the lady of his plantation and a northern captain. They are united at the end, as are North and South.

Even more popular than Page's were the "Uncle Remus" stories of the Georgian Joel Chandler Harris, which were collected in nine books, starting in 1880. Page drew on actual folktales, but his view of slavery was as imaginary as Page's. In one story, a loyal slave learns that Lee has surrendered. He steps across a line to see what it feels like to be free. "'T ain't needer no hotter ner no colder on dis side dan what 't is on dat," he announces. To his "marse" he quickly adds: "Don't you tell mistiss dat I been free, kaze she'll take a bresh-broom an' run me off'n de place when I get home."

The turn of the twentieth century brought even more virulent racism. Thomas Dixon's novels of 1902 and 1905, *The Leopard's Spots* and *The Clansman*, glorified the Klan for saving white women from black rapists. So did *The Birth of a Nation*, D. W. Griffith's 1915 movie based on the books.

Again, the surprise is not that this appealed to some southerners but that it did to so many northerners as well. But perhaps it's not so surprising—perhaps those who felt lost in the urban industrial North were all-the-more eager to escape into an agrarian romance, however fictional. And perhaps northerners also appreciated Page's willingness to make a Yankee as fine a gentleman as any southerner.

The best-known portrayal of a romantic South was, of course, *Gone With the Wind*. Margaret Mitchell's 1936 novel and the 1939 movie based on it were among a number of "southerns," a genre that never became as popular as the western but which included the 1938 *Jezebel* (starring Bette Davis) and the 1946 *Song of the South* (based on Joel Chandler Harris's Uncle Remus stories).

In the late twentieth and early twenty-first century, the continuing appeal of the Lost Cause could be seen in a spate of alternative histories in which the South wins the Civil War. Among the most popular of these were Harry Turtledove's series of eleven volumes (1997–2007) and Newt Gingrich and William R. Forstchen's series of three volumes (2003–2005). Turtledove's alternative history diverges from actual history when Lee wins at Antietam; Gingrich and Forstchen's diverges when Lee wins at Gettysburg. A 1992 stand-alone novel by Turtledove, *The Guns of the South,* combined alternative history with time travel; for this one, some white supremacists from an imagined twenty-first century South Africa supply the Confederates with AK-47s to help them win the war.

It's not just in these alternative histories that the war rages on—with the South winning. Reenactors still regularly don blue and gray uniforms, with more preferring the latter, for what one of them dubbed a "Civil Wargasm." Turn on the news and white supremacist rhetoric, sometimes but not always more coded than Dixon's, can still be heard loud and clear. In 2017, white supremacists rallied around a statue of Lee in Charlottesville, and one rammed his car into a crowd, killing a counter-protester. Lee and Jackson and Davis still stand tall on Richmond's Monument Avenue. In fact, according to a 2018 report in *Smithsonian Magazine,* over the previous ten years at least $40 million of taxpayer money had been spent on Confederate monuments, museums, cemeteries, and heritage organizations throughout the South.

But there have always been voices questioning the nobility of the Lost Cause, and these voices, too, can be heard. On Decoration Day in 1878, Frederick Douglass spoke in New York's Union Square before a statue of Lincoln, not Lee. "I admit that the South believed it was right," Douglass said. "but the nature of things is not changed by belief." This had been, he continued, a war between "slavery and freedom, barbarism and civilization; between a government based upon the broadest and grandest declaration of human rights the world ever heard or read, and another pretended government, based upon an open, bold, and shocking denial of rights." In 1931, W. E. B. Du Bois suggested that Confederate monuments ought to carry this inscription: "sacred to the memory of those who fought to Perpetuate Human Slavery."

In 2019, Richmond's Valentine Museum hosted an exhibit in which planners, architects, designers, and others presented their ideas for reimagining the city's Monument Avenue. Some of the proposals called for getting rid of the monuments. Some called for adding plaques providing historical context. And some were quite creative: One suggested depressing the monuments into the earth so that they could be viewed both from their original perspective and from a new one. Another suggested planting magnolia trees around them so that as the trees grew the monuments, though still there, would be gradually hidden. A third called for adding new monuments honoring those who fought for freedom.

Few of the proposals seemed realistic, financially or politically. But all had this in common: They suggested new ways of telling an American story.

CHAPTER EIGHTEEN

The Noble Outlaw

NO ONE'S REPUTATION BENEFITED MORE FROM THE LOST CAUSE THAN that of Jesse James. James played only a minor role in the Civil War. He was a bushwhacker, a term that described Confederates who fought as guerillas rather than as regular soldiers. He was certainly no Robert E. Lee or Stonewall Jackson. Yet in the postwar years, the southern press turned James—whose resume consisted primarily of robbing banks and trains—into a defender of southern honor, the bane of evil (northern) corporations, a nineteenth-century Robin Hood.

"Missouri leads [the country] . . . in the heroic splendor and perfect sangfroid of her gallant highwaymen," wrote the aptly named Missouri weekly, the *Lexington Weekly Caucasian*, in 1873. "These old bushwhackers never fail, and then their coolness . . . wins our admiration."

"We called him an outlaw . . . but fate made him so," wrote the *Sedalia Democrat*, another Missouri newspaper, in its 1882 obituary. "When the war closed Jesse James had no home. Proscribed, hunted, shot, driven away from among his people, a price put on his head—what else could the man do, with such a nature, except what he did do? . . . When he was hunted he turned savagely about and hunted his hunters."

Granted, James's fame rested on more than his bushwhacker background. His gang was among the first to rob banks during daylight and to rob trains at all, and they did so with a sense of drama that the press found irresistible (and, lest the press not fully appreciate their exploits, after one train robbery the gang left behind a printed press release). The authorities, who included the famous detective Allan Pinkerton, chased him for sixteen years but never caught him. "In all the history of medieval knight errantry and modern brigandage," the *Caucasian* boasted in 1874, "there is nothing that equals the wild romance of the past few years."

Jesse was no more the leader of the gang than his brother Frank. But Jesse had the charisma and the looks: "The blue eyes, very clear and penetrating, are never at rest," swooned the *St. Louis Dispatch* in 1874. "There is always a smile on his lips, and a graceful word or a compliment for all with whom he comes in contact. Looking at his small white hands, with their long tapering fingers, one would not imagine that with a revolver they were among the quickest and deadliest hands in all the west."

Like the *Dispatch*, we tend to think of James as a figure out of the Old West, but he was foremost a southerner. He grew up in a family of slaveholders in the border state of Missouri. There the Civil War consisted less of conventional battles than of guerilla attacks, with neighbors often murdering neighbors. In 1863, he witnessed Union troops interrogate his mother and stepfather (according to Confederate accounts, brutally). In 1864, when he was seventeen, he joined a group of bushwhackers led by "Bloody Bill" Anderson. He participated in several battles, including one in which Anderson's band murdered two dozen unarmed Union soldiers. He was shot (according to Confederate accounts, while he was attempting to surrender).

After the war, many of the bushwhackers turned to robbery. Their targets were sometimes but not always their wartime enemies. It's not clear when James recovered from his gunshot wound sufficiently to join them. He certainly participated in an 1869 robbery of the Daviess County Savings Association in Gallatin, Missouri. There he shot the bank's owner, John Sheets, whom James mistook for the Union officer who had killed Anderson.

The robbery and killing brought James to the attention of John Newman Edwards, a newspaperman devoted to the Lost Cause. Edwards took it upon himself to tell James's story, and Edwards played a major role in turning James into a legend. The passages quoted above from the *Sedalia Democrat* and the *St. Louis Dispatch* were both written by Edwards. Edwards may also have written or at least edited 1870 letters from James to the *Kansas City Times*; in these James proclaimed his innocence of robbery and murder but said he could not surrender because the authorities would not give a fair trial to someone who "fought under the black flag." The black flag, once a pirate symbol, now referred to bushwhackers.

An 1872 robbery at an industrial exposition in Kansas City, in which the James gang seized the cash box from the ticket window, drew more admiration from Edwards. His report in the *Kansas City Times* described the robbery as "one of those exhibitions of superb daring that chills the blood and transfixes the muscles of the looker-on." Edwards followed up with an editorial titled "The Chivalry of Crime," in which he waxed even more poetic. "These men sometimes rob," he asserted. "But it is always in the glare of the day and in the teeth of the multitude. . . . The nineteenth century . . . is not the soil for men who might have sat with Arthur at the Round Table, ridden with Sir Launcelot or worn the colors of Guinivere."

A couple of weeks later the *Kansas City Times* published a letter from James or some other gang member that was probably written or edited by Edwards. The writer signed off as Jack Shepherd, Dick Turpin, and Claude Duval—all legendary European bandits—and then made explicit the connection to the most famous robber hero of all: "We rob the rich and give to the poor." But even as he identified himself with Robin Hood, the letter writer made clear these robberies were motivated not by altruism but by the politics of Reconstruction. He could not resist a crack at the party of Lincoln: "Just let a party of men commit a bold robbery, and the cry is hang them," he wrote, "but Grant and his party can steal millions, and it is all right."

James's image as a Robin Hood was further enhanced in 1873, when he started robbing trains as well as banks. He supposedly checked passengers' hands to avoid taking anything from working men, and he was generally less interested in passengers' money than what was in the train's safe. Moreover, railroads were examples—and indeed symbols—of large corporations that operated without regard to their effect on small farmers. Railroads were also key to the nation's westward expansion, and by making them his target James transformed himself from a southern hero to a western (and national) hero. But even then, he was very much still an ex-bushwhacker; after at least one train robbery, witnesses described the robbers as wearing masks like those of the Ku Klux Klan.

In 1875, Pinkerton's men thought they had the James brothers trapped inside the family's farmhouse. The detectives tossed through a window a device that was intended to illuminate the scene, or possibly to set the house on fire and force out the Jameses. Instead, it exploded, injuring the James's mother and killing their younger half-brother. Jesse and Frank, it turned out, weren't in the house.

Pinkerton was unapologetic, later calling James "the worst man, without exception in America," one who "has no more compunction about cold blooded murder than he has about eating his breakfast." But believers in the Lost Cause saw the raid on the house—and the killing of the James's young brother—as further evidence that Jesse James was a victim of northern persecution.

Though Pinkerton never got his man, Jesse James was not invincible. An 1876 robbery of a bank in Northfield, Minnesota, went awry, and three members of the gang were wounded and captured. Their replacements, including a teenager named Robert Ford, were less trustworthy. In April 1882 Ford, hoping for a reward, shot Jesse James in the back and killed him. Ford was convicted of murder and then pardoned. Frank James surrendered to the governor in October and was charged with robbery and murder but never convicted.

Despite the efforts of Edwards and others to portray him as a Robin Hood, Jesse James did not rob from the rich and give to the poor. He may have robbed from the rich, but he did not give to the poor. He may have focused on safes rather than passengers, but that's because the safes held more money. He may have paid well those who provided his gang with horses and food and other supplies, but that's not the same as giving to the poor. He may sometimes have sought to right wrongs, but the wrongs he cared about were those committed against white southerners, and the cause he cared about was their Lost Cause.

"James was not an . . . avenger for the poor," wrote his most recent (and best) biographer, T. J. Stiles. "His popularity was driven by politics . . . and was rooted among former Confederates. Even his attacks on unpopular economic targets, the banks and the railroads, turn out on closer inspection to have had political resonances."

"Had Jesse James existed a century later," Stiles asserted, "he would have been called a terrorist."

The Robin Hood version of James's life, however, was well established before historians could weigh in with their evidence. Indeed, even before he died and then even more so in the following years, James's legend was widely spread by inexpensive paperbacks known as dime novels. In the late nineteenth and early twentieth century, there were more dime novels published about Jesse James than about any other figure except Buffalo Bill. Not only did these books portray the brothers as good guys, but some went so far as to have them capture the real bad guys; witness, for example, *The James Boys and Pinkerton; or Frank and Jesse as Detectives*. (This was #39 in a series of 803 dime novels titled *The New York Detective Library* and published between 1883 and 1898, and this was just one of several series that featured Jesse James.) In books like these, James was almost a precursor of the twentieth century's hardboiled detectives—men who operated outside the law but with a clear moral code.

Nonfiction books of the nineteenth century (or, rather, books that claimed to be nonfiction) tended to follow the lead of Edwards's newspaper articles. At least three books about James and his gang were published in 1880, two years before his death, and Frank Triplett's *The Life, Times and Treacherous Death of Jesse James* came out a month after the death. Triplett claimed his book was based on interviews with James's widow and mother. James's widow disowned the book, but that did not stop her from suing the publisher for her share of the royalties. Edwards himself weighed in with *Noted Guerillas, or Warfare of the Border*, in 1877.

James's son, Jesse Edwards James (his middle name may have come from the newspaper editor who promoted his father) published *Jesse James, My Father* in 1899. This was the first book to include an often-repeated story in which Jesse James, flush with cash from a recent robbery, stops at a farmhouse for a meal. There he finds a tearful widow who tells him her house and farm are about to be foreclosed by a banker. James gives her the money she needs and leaves. The banker arrives and is disappointed he can't take the property but greedily accepts the cash. He

THE NEW YORK

PRICE TEN CENTS.

Detective Library.

No. 373. { COMPLETE. } FRANK TOUSEY, PUBLISHER, 34 & 36 NORTH MOORE STREET, N.Y. { PRICE } Vol. I.
NEW YORK, JANUARY 18, 1890. { 10 CENTS. }

The Subscription Price of The New York Detective Library is $5.00 per year. Money should be sent by Post Office Money Order or Registered Letter. Address
FRANK TOUSEY, Publisher, 34 and 36 North Moore Street, New York. Box 2730.

OLD SADDLE-BAGS, THE PREACHER DETECTIVE;

OR,

THE JAMES BOYS IN A FIX.

By D. W. STEVENS.

Old Saddle Bags, 1890.

LIBRARY OF CONGRESS

leaves the farm to return to the bank and encounters James, who robs him of the money. Similar stories had long circulated about other outlaws, so this was most likely a folktale.

Folk songs about James also spread the legend. One ballad that probably originated soon after James's death used Howard, an alias of James, in a chorus that included the line, "that dirty little coward that shot Mister Howard." Among those who recorded versions of the song were Woody Guthrie, Pete Seeger, Johnny Cash, and Bruce Springsteen.

Movies about James included two in which Jesse Edwards James starred as his father; both of these, *Jesse James Under the Black Flag* and *Jesse James as the Outlaw*, were released in 1921. In 1939, *Jesse James* starred Tyrone Power as Jesse and Henry Fonda as Frank. The brothers are forced to turn to crime after a railroad agent, eager to seize their farm, kills their mother. The movie was a hit and led a year later to a sequel, *The Return of Frank James*, as well as to numerous other films about noble outlaws, including the 1941 *Billy the Kid*.

In 1957, *The True Story of Jesse James*, directed by Nicholas Ray and starring Robert Wagner, presented James's life of crime as a result of youthful traumas, placing the movie in the same genre as the 1955 *Rebel without a Cause* (also directed by Ray). Darker depictions followed, including Robert Duvall's in the 1972 *The Great Northfield Minnesota Raid* and Brad Pitt's in the 2007 *The Assassination of Jesse James by the Coward Robert Ford*. The latter, though based on Ron Hansen's 1983 novel of the same name, offered a historically credible (albeit speculative) view of James and Ford. But lest one think history has triumphed over myth, in 2001 there was *American Outlaws*, which starred Colin Farrell as a Jesse James more like Tyrone Power's than Brad Pitt's. Evaluating the historical accuracy of *American Outlaws*, wrote Stiles, "is about as pointless as a discussion of the differences between bumper cars and highway driving." More generally, historian Richard White wrote, "in popular culture . . . the American West might as well be Sherwood Forest."

Chapter Nineteen

Steel-Driving Man

What most people know of John Henry comes from the ballad that took his name. Though there are many variations of the ballad, by 1910 or so the story most of them told had certain elements in common.

As a baby, John Henry predicts he will become a "steel-driving man." This was someone who struck a steel drill with a heavy hammer in order to make a hole; railroad workers then inserted explosives in these holes and blasted tunnels through mountains. The baby or little boy also predicts that this work "is going to be the death of me."

His prophecies come true. As an adult, John Henry becomes a powerful steel driver for the railroad, so powerful that sometime in the early 1870s he agrees to race a newly invented steam drill to see who can dig deeper. John Henry wins the race but the effort is too much even for him and he dies, either right then and there or soon after.

As the ballad spread, John Henry became a symbol of almost superhuman strength. His story appealed especially to African American workers since in many versions he was a freed slave. It appealed to other workers as well, since John Henry, faced with a steam drill and more generally with industrialization, insisted on his humanity. "A man," he proclaimed in many versions, "ain't nothin' but a man."

In the 1920s, a sociologist named Guy Johnson and an English professor named Lewis Chappell independently took it upon themselves to track the story back to its origins. It was by no means clear they would find a real John Henry. However exaggerated were the deeds of, say Davy Crockett, no one doubted he existed. But the documentary record for

African Americans was much more meager than for whites, and fifty years had passed before Johnson and Chappell began interviewing people who might have had first- or even second-hand knowledge of John Henry. Often, it was impossible to tell whether people were remembering an actual event or the story in the ballad. There were stories of John Henry racing a steam drill everywhere from Birmingham to Santa Fe. It wasn't even clear whether Henry was a last name or a middle name.

Nevertheless, both Johnson and Chappell concluded the story was based on fact. Johnson admitted there was a "mountain of negative evidence," but he still leaned toward believing in John Henry, and Chappell was adamant about the story being true. Both Johnson and Chappell found a great many of those they interviewed placed the race at the site of the Big Bend Tunnel, which the C&O Railroad (originally the Covington & Ohio and later the Chesapeake & Ohio) had built in West Virginia between 1869 and 1872.

Whatever the origins of the story, songs about John Henry dated back to very soon after he supposedly died. Before the ballad, there were "hammer songs." These were sung by men building railroads and they served to set and keep a rhythm as they worked. One went:

> If I could drive steel like John Henry,
> I'd go home, Baby, I'd go home.

Chants like these, broken up with blows from hammers, were also sung by miners and by chain gangs throughout the South.

Keeping a steady rhythm was a matter of life and death for the steel driver's partner, who was called a shaker or turner and who rotated the drill after each blow. If the shaker moved his hands at the wrong moment, the driver's hammer could crush it. For railroad workers and miners, the words of some hammer songs must have served as a warning and perhaps a prayer. A stanza from another hammer song went:

> This old hammer
> Killed John Henry;

It won't kill me, boys,
It won't kill me.

The hammer songs may have evolved into ballads, or the ballads may have evolved independently. In any case, for more than three decades from the early 1870s, workers transmitted and transformed the ballad orally.

Soon after the turn of the century, folklore scholars began to track and transcribe the song, culminating in the work of Johnson and Chappell. The poet Carl Sandburg sang a version of the ballad and in 1927 included it in his popular book, *The American Songbag*, and John and Alan Lomax included it in their various and very popular collections of folk songs.

The ballad was especially popular among African American and blues singers, including W. C. Handy and Leadbelly. But it appealed to whites as well. Folk singers including Burl Ives, Woody Guthrie, and Pete Seeger made it a standard item in their repertoires. The ballad was also sung by Tennessee Ernie Ford, Johnny Cash, Bruce Springsteen, and by others as gospel and country and rock.

The elliptical nature of the song allowed singers and listeners to see it as about many things. John Henry was usually black but sometimes white. He was embraced by those who saw the railroads as a symbol of the dehumanizing industrialization of America— indeed, some saw him as just as much of an anti-railroad symbol as Jesse James—but he also came to be loved by railroad buffs. Socialists and communists sang the ballad but so did racists: In fact, the first record labeled "John Henry" came in 1924 from Fiddlin' John Carson, a member of the Ku Klux Klan.

Wrote historian Scott Reynolds Nelson: "John Henry was appropriated to tell the story about the position of black men during Jim Crow, about the pains of the life of [railroad workers], about the dangers of mining, . . . about the coming of the machine age, about nostalgia for the past, about the terrors of textile mills, about capitalism, and about the Black Power movement." Above all, though, it was "a story of courage in conflict with power."

Freudians as well as Marxists found much in the ballad to analyze. As early as 1933, Chappell noted the sexual connotations of steel drills and tunnels, and he included in his book variations of the ballad that were more explicit about John Henry's sex life. For example:

> When the women heard of John Henry's death
> They all dressed up in red.   When the people ask them
> where they were going,
> "We are going where John Henry fell dead."

In his 1960 collection of folk songs, Lomax noted that the ballad asserted that "men are always more important than the machines they build" and quickly added: "Every singer knows, consciously or unconsciously, that John Henry could prove this by night as well as by day."

In many variations of the ballad, John Henry has a lover or a wife, often but not always named Polly Ann. In some, she even picks up his hammer after his death and—a la Molly Pitcher—starts driving steel herself. But in others, she too has many lovers. Went one:

> John Henry had a lovin' little wife,
> Always went dressed in blue.
> Every time John Henry was gone away from home
> She goes out with the steel-driving crew.

Though he appeared most often in songs, John Henry also found his way into other art forms. During the 1930s he was a regular presence in collections of folk stories and on socialist and communist posters. The white muralist Frank W. Long produced one of the most striking images of a gigantic John Henry.

Roark Bradford's supposedly comic novel, *John Henry*, was published in 1931. Bradford's John Henry draws on stereotypical ideas of black dialogue and character. The book was nonetheless chosen by the Literary Guild, which noted that its white author "is amply qualified to write about the Negro" because "he was born on a plantation" and "had a Negro for a nurse and Negroes for playmates when he was growing up" and "has

John Henry by Frank W. Long. Long gave the image to a Lexington, Kentucky, student in 1941 as a high school art award.

COLLECTION OF WARREN AND JULIE PAYNE

seen them at work in the fields." Bradford turned the novel into a musical play starring Paul Robeson. It flopped.

The civil rights movement turned John Henry into an inspirational hero of a number of children's and young adult books, including Ezra Keats's *John Henry: An American Legend* in 1965 and John Oliver Killens's *A Man Ain't Nothin but a Man* in 1975. In 1972 a statue of John Henry was placed in Talcott, West Virginia, near the Big Bend Tunnel.

In the 1990s, a superhero named Steel appeared alongside Superman in comic books. His real name was John Henry Irons. In the 1997 movie, *Steel*, basketball player Shaquille O'Neal had the title role.

The most ambitious literary work featuring John Henry was Colson Whitehead's 2001 novel, *John Henry Days*. Whitehead wove together the stories of Henry and various others, primarily a current-day freelance writer named J. Sutter. Unlike Roark's novel, Whitehead's is genuinely funny. J. goes to West Virginia to cover a festival commemorating John Henry but mostly to pad his expense account and take advantage of the free food and drink. He is also out to set the record for the most consecutive days attending a publicity event. John Henry and J. seem to have little in common, but Whitehead makes clear both are struggling to define manhood in dehumanizing worlds. Like those who had taken the folk song and made it their own, Whitehead did not try to uncover the historical figure. Rather, as one of his characters said about the songwriters, "You mix it up, cut a verse or two and stick to the verses that you like or remember or mean something to you. Then you've assembled your own John Henry."

Historian Scott Nelson, however, continued to search for the real John Henry. He came upon an old photo of the Virginia Penitentiary and noticed that one of the buildings was white and that train tracks ran by the prison. This brought to his mind a stanza from one version of the ballad:

> They took John Henry to the white house
> And buried him in the san'
> And every locomotive come roarin' by
> Says there lays that steel drivin' man . . .

Investigating further, Nelson found a list of prisoners that included a John William Henry. He also learned that about three hundred skeletons had been found in an area of the prison near the railroad tracks.

Again from prison records Nelson learned that the Virginia Penitentiary had rented out inmates to work on the C&O Railroad, and that John William Henry had been one of these prisoners. From the C&O's engineering reports, he learned that steam drills had not been used at the Big Bend Tunnel but that they had been tested against men at the nearby Lewis Tunnel. The prison records confirmed Henry had been one of the prisoners sent to work at the Lewis Tunnel.

The prison records did not indicate what happened to Henry; they noted only that he had been "transferred." Nelson surmised that prisoners had been buried near the white house to cover up how many had died working for the railroad. Most were killed by lung diseases caused by hazardous dust they had inhaled working in the tunnel.

Nelson's conclusion—a convincing one—was that John William Henry was the real John Henry. This John Henry was African American (the prison records included a "c" for "colored"), but he was not a freed slave; rather, he was a free man from New Jersey. He was not the giant of lore but was just over five feet one inch tall. He was nineteen years old in 1866 when he entered the prison, having been found guilty of robbing twenty dollars' worth of goods from a store. Under Virginia's harsh "black codes," he had been sentenced to ten years in prison. For John William Henry, Nelson commented, that turned out to be a death sentence.

CHAPTER TWENTY

The Wild West

WILLIAM CODY, BETTER KNOWN AS BUFFALO BILL, WAS A VERY MODERN kind of celebrity. He was more famous for being himself than for anything he did. He rode for the Pony Express, hunted buffalo, scouted for the army, and fought Indians, but much of his life was spent promoting what he'd done.

To be sure, other western heroes had also promoted themselves. Daniel Boone worked with John Filson on Filson's book about Boone's exploits. Davy Crockett told plenty of tall tales about himself in his books and on the campaign trail. But Boone had played a key role in settling Kentucky and Crockett had fought at the Alamo, even if he didn't die there. Cody, in contrast, would be remembered as a pretty minor figure in western history—had he not founded and starred in the wildly successful show known as *Buffalo Bill's Wild West*.

This huge outdoor pageant reenacted scenes from Cody's life as well as other supposedly typical scenes of western life, such as one in which a settler family's cabin is attacked by Indians. The settlers' situation looks hopeless until, at the last moment, a posse of cowboys rides to the rescue led by none other than Buffalo Bill himself. Cody certainly looked the part of the hero. He had long, flowing hair, a handlebar mustache, and a goatee. "Central casting couldn't have imagined a better actor," wrote Deanne Stillman, whose nonfiction works have been set in the historical and modern West. "He was oh so handsome; his long flowing hair rendered him both rugged and ethereal."

In the late nineteenth and early twentieth century, *Buffalo Bill's Wild West* performed in front of audiences totaling more than fifty million people throughout America and Europe. The show featured hundreds of cowboys and Indians, horses and buffalo, all traveling by train and ship and so efficiently that the staff of the imperial German army studied its methods of loading and unloading.

Which of Cody's stories were real and which were invented?

To start with, it's unclear whether he ever rode for the Pony Express. In his 1879 autobiography, Cody claimed to have joined when he was thirteen years old, and the next year to have teamed up with the lawman and gunfighter Wild Bill Hickok to track down some Indians who had shut down the mail service by attacking a stagecoach and stealing horses. But Cody could not have joined in 1859 as he claimed, since the Pony Express was not launched until 1860, and the Indian attack on the stagecoach he described didn't take place until 1862, by which time the Pony Express was no longer operating. In the absence of corroborating witnesses, doubts about Cody's Pony Express stories are reasonable. The essential truth Cody grasped, however, was that the Pony Express was a perfect symbol for a westward-moving nation. It would be an extremely popular part of his show about winning the West.

Hunting, too, was key to his image. Boone and Crockett were famed for their hunting and so was Cody. Cody's prey was buffalo (hence his nickname), and buffalo hunts were another part of the Wild West show. In the show, Cody used blanks, and his captive herd helped preserve the species. But before then he had done his part to drive buffalo near to extinction. In 1867 and 1868, he was employed by the Kansas Pacific Railroad to hunt buffalo to feed workers building tracks to the West. He claimed to have shot 4,280 buffalo for the railroad, including sixty in one afternoon.

Later, when easterners could ride the railroad to the West, Cody led hunting parties of wealthy sportsmen who wanted the thrill of mounting horses and chasing buffalo across the plains. The most famous of these tourists was Russia's Grand Duke Alexie, the son of the tsar. In 1872, Cody led Alexei toward a herd. Alexei wasn't much of a shot, and Cody had to urge the grand duke's horse close to the buffalo and tell him when to shoot. That worked, and Alexei was thrilled.

"We gave him three cheers, and . . . we took a pull at the champagne in honor of the Grand Duke's success," Cody wrote in his autobiography. "I was in hopes that he would kill five or six more buffaloes before we reached camp, especially if a basket of champagne was to be opened every time he dropped one."

In acting as a guide for tourists, Cody was rehearsing a role he would later flesh out. Sitting by the campfire, he would tell tales of his adventures, and his guests could feel they were a part of them.

Some of those adventures were as a scout for the US Cavalry, which employed Cody between 1868 and 1872. As a scout, Cody participated in sixteen battles with Indians. And like Boone and Crockett, he also understood Indian ways and was not afraid to venture into their territory alone, with his horse as his only companion.

"He may not really have been a *great* scout," wrote Larry McMurtry, the novelist and essayist whose work is mostly set in the Old West. "He could not claim to have traveled the great reach of territory that Kit Carson, Jedediah Smith . . . or the Delaware scout Black Beaver all mastered. But he was a better horseman than any of the above—it is entirely fitting that in the poster art created for his shows he is nearly always on horseback."

Added McMurtry: "It is hard to overestimate how far a man can go in America if he looks good on a horse."

Cody's fame as a hunter and a scout spread via dime novels. The first of these was *Buffalo Bill, the King of the Border Men*, which first appeared in serial form in the *New York Weekly* in 1869. It was written by Edward Zane Carroll Judson, who wrote under the pen name Ned Buntline and later partnered with Cody in *Buffalo Bill's Wild West*. Buffalo Bill himself was credited as author of twenty-five dime novels, though whether he actually wrote them is unclear. Many historians doubted he even read them. Cody's sister, Helen Cody Wetmore, said he did write them but noted that her brother did not share some of the usual author's concerns:

"Life is too short," Cody said (according to Wetmore), "to make big letters when small ones will do; and as for punctuation, if my readers don't know enough to take their breath without those little marks, they'll have to lose it, that's all."

Cody's attitude toward some of the details in his plots was equally unfussy. "I am sorry to have lied so outrageously in this yarn," he wrote to a publisher (again according to Wetmore). "My hero has killed more Indians in one war-trail than I have killed in all my life. But I understand that is what is expected in border tales. If you think the revolver and bowie-knife are used too freely, you may cut out a fatal shot or stab wherever you deem it wise."

Buntline turned his first dime novel about Cody into a play, and *Buffalo Bill, the King of the Border Men* opened in New York in 1872 with Cody present on opening night. The audience cheered him, just as an audience had cheered Crockett when he attended a play about himself in 1833. Unlike Crockett, Cody seized the opportunity to cash in on his fame by playing himself. Later in 1872, Cody became the star of a new play, *The Scouts of the Plains*. The author was the prolific Buntline, who said he'd written the play in four hours.

On opening night in Chicago, Cody completely forgot his lines. The versatile Buntline, who was appearing in the play he'd written, improvised. He asked Buffalo Bill where he'd been. Cody answered he'd been hunting and proceeded to tell stories about his adventures. "In this way, I took up fifteen minutes, without once speaking a word of my part," Cody recalled in his autobiography, "nor did I speak a word of it during the whole evening."

The plot made little sense. Cody rescued an Indian maiden who spoke with an Italian accent because she was played by an Italian dancer. Much of the play consisted of Buffalo Bill blazing away at various Indians. "We would kill them all off in one act," Cody recalled, "but they would come up again ready for business in the next." Wrote the *Chicago Tribune*: "Such a combination of incongruous drama, execrable acting, renowned performers, mixed audience, intolerable stanch, scalping, blood and thunder, is not likely to be vouchsafed to a city a second time, even Chicago." The *Chicago Times* commented that if Buntline had spent four hours writing the play, it was difficult to see what he had been doing all that time.

No matter: The play was a hit.

For the next ten years, Cody would split his time between acting in plays that toured the East and acting as a guide for hunting parties or as a scout for the army in the West. In *The Scouts of the Prairie*, which was otherwise much like *The Scouts of the Plains*, Buffalo Bill was joined on stage by Wild Bill Hickok. The pairing lasted only through the 1873-1874 season, partly because Hickok got carried away during some of the fight scenes and the actors playing the Indians complained they were getting hurt.

Cody's new adventures out west were quickly incorporated into plays back east. This was the case with his most famous Indian fight, which took place after George Armstrong Custer's disastrous defeat at Little Bighorn in June 1876. Cody was not with Custer at Little Bighorn, but he was acting as an army scout ten days later when he and fifteen other scouts encountered a band of Cheyenne. What happened next was the basis for *The Red Right Hand, or the First Scalp for Custer*, a play that opened before the year was out.

As Cody described the fight in his autobiography, one of the Indians, a chief named Yellow Hand, rode back and forth in front of his men and spoke directly to Cody, telling him he knew who he was and "if you want to fight, come ahead and fight me." Cody accepted the challenge, and the two galloped toward each other at full speed. When they were about thirty feet apart, Cody fired and killed the Indian's horse, but his own horse stepped into a hole and also fell to the ground. Indian and scout were now both on foot, and they fired at each other simultaneously.

"My usual luck did not desert me," Cody wrote, "for his bullet missed me, while mine struck him in the breast." Before Yellow Hand had even touched the ground, Cody drove his knife into his heart. Then: "Jerking his war-bonnet off, I scientifically scalped him in about five seconds." He swung the prize in the air and shouted, "The first scalp for Custer." The rest of the Indians soon retreated.

Helen Wetmore Cody called the fight with Yellow Hand a "duel," adding to the sense that this was a confrontation between two important leaders. The duel with Yellow Hand became a key part of the Cody legend, not just in the play that opened later that year but as reenacted in *Buffalo Bill's Wild West*. It established Cody as a man an Indian chief saw worthy of singling out, and as the man who avenged Custer.

As with so many stories about Buffalo Bill, this was based on an actual event but Cody's role was much exaggerated. Witnesses confirm that on July 17, 1786, Cody did participate in a battle with Cheyenne near what's today the Nebraska-Wyoming border, and he did kill an Indian. But the Indian was named Yellow Hair and not Yellow Hand, and he was not an important chief. None of the witnesses other than Cody mentioned Yellow Hair challenging Cody to fight one-on-one, and since Cody and Yellow Hair didn't speak each other's languages, it seems unlikely they spoke to each other at all. If the Indians paid special attention to Cody, it was probably because he dressed in a way that he was sure to be noticed. He was wearing a suit of black velvet slashed with scarlet and trimmed with silver buttons and lace; this was a costume he had worn on stage before and would wear on stage again when he reenacted the fight for audiences back east. The fight itself was a fairly minor skirmish, and since Yellow Hair had not been at Little Bighorn, it's hard to see his as "the first scalp for Custer."

The novels and the shows were merely prelude to the show that made Cody perhaps the most famous man in America. The show began in 1882 as part of a Fourth of July celebration in Nebraska featuring displays of marksmanship, riding, and roping. Soon Cody added scenes like the Indian attack on the settlers' cabin and an Indian attack on a stagecoach (again rescued by Cody) and the duel with Yellow Hand. There were also cowboy bands, horse races, and buffalo hunts, and starting in 1885 actual Indians instead of actors playing Indians. Some of the many circuses touring in the 1880s included some of these elements, and the showman P. T. Barnum even tried, unsuccessfully, to stage a buffalo hunt. But none except Buffalo Bill's managed to convince audiences they were visiting the Wild West.

Besides Cody, the show's biggest star was Annie Oakley. Born Phoebe Ann Mosey, she and her husband Frank Butler performed together in theaters and circuses until she joined *Buffalo Bill's Wild West* in 1884. She was a sure shot with a pistol or a rifle or shotgun. In one performance, she shot a ten-cent piece out of the hand of an attendant thirty feet away. In another, she broke 4,772 of 5,000 glass balls fifteen yards away. She would enter an arena blowing kisses to the audience, and the audience loved her. She stayed with the show for sixteen years.

Almost as great an attraction as Annie Oakley was Sitting Bull, who joined *Buffalo Bill's Wild West* in 1885. Like Yellow Hair, Sitting Bull did not fight at Little Bighorn; unlike Yellow Hair, Sitting Bull was an important Lakota chief and a leader of the resistance to the United States's expansion. His role in the show was merely to trot around the arena on his horse while wearing his war bonnet and traditional clothing, but this was enough to excite the crowd.

Sitting Bull stayed with the show only a few months, but he and Cody became friends. A photograph of the two was sometimes captioned: "Foes in '76—Friends in '85." In fact, when rumors spread in 1890 that Sitting Bull might leave the reservation on which he was living and join the resistance to the army, the army summoned Cody west to talk the chief out of waging war. He was delayed, or rather waylaid by government agents who thought they could better handle the situation without him, and Sitting Bull was shot and killed. Some witnesses reported that Sitting Bull's horse, which had performed in *Buffalo Bill's Wild West*, heard the shots, recognized them as a cue from the show, and raised his front hooves to the sky.

In 1887 Cody took the show to England, where it played before the royal family. One oft-repeated story had the Prince of Wales and the kings of Denmark, Greece, Saxony, and Belgium in the stagecoach during the scene when the Indians attack, with Buffalo Bill driving the coach. The prince, who apparently played some poker, quipped that Buffalo Bill might never have held four kings before. Cody responded that four kings and the Prince of Wales made a royal flush. The story is dubious—witnesses recalled the prince and the king of Denmark on the coach but no others—but the show was a hit with both the royal family and the British public. The show regularly toured Europe until 1906.

"Sitting Bull and Buffalo Bill."

PHOTOGRAPH BY WILLIAM NOTMAN, 1885, LATER COPYRIGHTED BY D. F. BARRY, 1897. LIBRARY OF CONGRESS

The show's turn toward the rest of the world was reflected in some of its content as well. In 1893, "Rough Riders" from throughout the world joined cowboys and Indians on horseback; these included Cossacks, Mexicans, and Arabs. In 1899, Cody replaced a reenactment of Custer's battle with one of the 1898 Battle of San Juan Hill, in which Teddy Roosevelt's "Rough Riders" won a decisive victory over Spanish forces in Cuba. (Roosevelt claimed his Rough Riders weren't named after Cody's, but the show was so famous that's hard to believe.)

By 1906, however, the show's popularity and profitability was starting to decline. Cody brought back some of the frontier elements he'd dropped, such as Custer's battle, but that didn't help. Some of the problems stemmed from management mistakes. Others were the result of the gradually increasing popularity of movies, which could more effectively stage scenes like those in *Buffalo Bill's Wild West*.

Cody tried to shift some of his entrepreneurial energies into movies. Thomas Edison had filmed parts of his show in the 1890s, and Cody filmed parts in 1910 and 1911. In 1912, Cody starred in *The Life of Buffalo Bill*, in which an elderly Cody dreams of his adventures as a young man. In 1913, Cody produced and directed a movie about Indian wars of which only segments have survived. It flopped at the box office, which added to Cody's financial problems. Cody's other investments, which included mines and oil wells and a town named after him in Wyoming, also proved to be failures. When he died in 1917, he was broke.

Other actors went on to play Cody in the movies, including Roy Rogers in *Young Buffalo Bill* in 1940, Charlton Heston in *Pony Express* in 1953, and Paul Newman in *Buffalo Bill and the Indians, or Sitting Bull's History Lesson* in 1976. Rogers and Heston played heroes. Newman's Buffalo Bill was a drunk and a fraud.

Oakley went to the movies as well. Barbara Stanwyck starred in *Annie Oakley* in 1935 and Betty Hutton starred in *Annie Get Your Gun* in 1950. Ethel Merman had played Annie in the Broadway version of *Annie Get Your Gun*, which opened in 1946. *Annie Get Your Gun* was a musical whose hit songs were composed by Irving Berlin. Oakley's movie legacy also included complimentary tickets being named "Annie Oakleys," because the holes in the tickets resembled a bullet-ridden card.

Despite Cody's failure to profit from movies, he certainly influenced them. Much of what became standard in westerns originated with *Buffalo Bill's Wild West*. For decades, movie cowboys and Indians dressed and acted as they did in Cody's show. *Buffalo Bill's Wild West* defined how Americans saw their West . . . and their history.

In 1893, while the show played in Chicago, a history professor from the University of Wisconsin presented a paper in that same city.

"Up to our own day," said Frederick Jackson Turner, "American history has been in large degree the history of the colonization of the Great West." The frontier, Turner argued, had defined the American character, creating a people fiercely protective of their liberties. But in 1890, Turner noted, the superintendent of the census had found that so many settlements had broken up unsettled areas that a frontier line could no longer be discerned. Now, Turner concluded, "four centuries from the discovery of America, . . . the frontier has gone."

The West of *Buffalo Bill's Wild West* was already fading into history when Cody launched the show. It was gone by the time the show closed. And even before the Old West was gone, Americans were longing for it.

The Civil War had ended, but it was still difficult to see a heroic destiny manifested in the union of North and South. But East and West—there was a story that could unite Americans. Not all Americans, of course; Native Americans were no more enthusiastic about the history portrayed in *Buffalo Bill's Wild West* than African Americans were about the Lost Cause. But for most Americans, this West was an America to be celebrated.

So, perhaps, the question posed earlier in this chapter—What was real and what was invented?—is not the right question. The questions this book has explored are different ones—Why were certain stories invented and why did they spread? Buffalo Bill's portrayal of the Wild West spread far and wide, because it portrayed Americans the way Americans wanted to see themselves.

The programs for *Buffalo Bill's Wild West* always emphasized how authentic everything was. Indeed, publicists for the show never used the word *show*; rather, this was an exhibition or an educational experience.

These were real cowboys and real Indians, they stressed, and this was the real Buffalo Bill.

The publicists were wrong, of course. *Buffalo Bill's Wild West* was very much a show. The scenes it presented of Cody's life and of the West were full of exaggerations and outright fictions. But the show was also a brilliant artistic achievement, one that Cody's biographer Louis S. Warren compared to the works of D. W. Griffith, Eugene O'Neill, and Orson Welles.

It's unlikely very many in the audience for *Buffalo Bill's Wild West* were also in the audience for Frederick Jackson Turner's paper, but that didn't mean they didn't sense that their future would be a lot more urban than what they saw in the show, and that their future jobs, if not their current ones, were likely to be in offices or factories.

No wonder they dreamed of being cowboys.

FINAL THOUGHTS

WHY HAVE WE TOLD—AND BELIEVED—SO MANY MYTHS ABOUT AMERican history?

Sometimes it was sheer ignorance on the part of historians. The Reverend Jedidiah Morse, an active member of the American Historical Society and the author in 1784 of the children's book *Geography Made Easy*, confidently asserted that the highest mountains in North America were the Allegheny Mountains. This was perhaps forgivable in an era when the United States didn't extend much beyond the East Coast and when, as historian Frances Fitzgerald wrote, the clergymen who wrote for children had little background in history and "instead of trying to compensate for this deficiency they tended to make things up."

Less forgivable are the racist rantings of Jedidiah's son. Samuel Morse, as we have seen, was moved to commemorate a fictitious landing on Plymouth Rock at least in part because of his fears that the Pilgrims were being displaced by Catholic immigrants, as he made clear in his 1835 *Foreign Conspiracy Against the Liberties of the United States*. William Dunning, a president of the American Historical Association, was equally racist. Dunning, you may recall, was quoted in the preface to this book because of his insight as to how often historical errors not only pervade history but change its course. Dunning's work was a prime example of this. As a leading historian of the Lost Cause, he actively undercut African American rights on the grounds that "the freedmen were not . . . on the same social, moral, and intellectual plane with the whites."

So: Ignorance and prejudice have certainly spread myths about American history. What Richard Hofstadter in 1964 called "the paranoid style in American politics" has manifested itself in all sorts of conspiracy theories in which, to name just a few, the conspirators undermining

America have been Masons, Catholics, Jews, communists, and more recently a "deep state."

Americans have been particularly susceptible to fake news (and fake history), the cultural critic Kurt Andersen argued in his 2017 book *Fantasyland*, because of our faith in individualism. "Being American means we can believe any damn thing we want, that our beliefs are equal or superior to anyone else's," wrote Andersen. "The credible becomes incredible and the incredible credible."

In the late twentieth and early twenty-first centuries, the Internet made it even easier to believe in the incredible. There's almost no "fact" that can't be confirmed on some website. "The result," continued Andersen, "is the America we inhabit today, where reality and fantasy are weirdly and dangerously blurred."

But a few words in defense of fantasy.

The stories whose evolutions are traced in this book were stories that united Americans. We could all celebrate a president who even as a child could not tell a lie, or a child who grew up to be president even though he was born in a log cabin. We could all admire the courage and curiosity that propelled Americans westward. We could all enjoy a Thanksgiving feast.

Well, not all, of course. These stories tended to leave out a good deal of history. Women got short shrift. Native Americans and African Americans got even worse. Some of these stories were purely pernicious: It did not take much of a leap to go from believing in the Lost Cause to supporting the Ku Klux Klan.

But if we can recognize that the stories we have told about American history are often untrue and always incomplete, we can perhaps still find in some of them much to believe in. Imagine Pilgrims and Indians sitting down together in peace. Imagine spreading apple seeds across the land. Imagine a land of opportunity for all. Imagine a president who cannot tell a lie.

Much of this is beyond our imagination, so fully have debunkers punctured our fantasies. And more recent stories—the stories that grew out of twentieth- and twenty-first-century history—were very different from the earlier ones. Instead of uniting us, these new stories increasingly reflected and reinforced divisions in America, with each side willing to implicate the other in sordid conspiracies.

Pearl Harbor? Franklin Roosevelt knew the Japanese were going to attack and suppressed that knowledge in order to force America to go to war. The atom bomb? Harry Truman knew the Japanese would have surrendered anyway, but he dropped the bomb to send a message to Moscow, and thus began the Cold War. The assassination of John F. Kennedy? Lee Harvey Oswald didn't act alone; this was a conspiracy involving the FBI, or the CIA, or the Mafia, or someone else. 9/11? Blame not Al-Qaeda but Israel, or Saudi Arabia, or the US government itself.

These twentieth- and twenty-first-century myths are beyond the scope of this book. But, immersed as we are in stories that divide us, I hope it has been a bit refreshing to trace the evolution of some earlier stories—stories that united us and made us proud to be Americans.

If some of these stories are not so much histories as "wishtories," so be it.

Acknowledgments

I am grateful for the advice of Marc Leepson, Edward Lengel, John Thorn, and especially Stephen Aron. Thanks also to my agent, John Thornton, Copyeditor Josh Rosenberg, Layout Artist Wanda Ditch, Cover Designer Sally Rinehart, Proofreader Anita Oliva, Indexer Kathleen Rocheleau, Production Editor Alex Bordelon, and especially Editorial Director Gene Brissie.

Source Notes

Preface

"The Cannot-Tell-a-Lie . . ." W. E. Woodward, *George Washington: The Image and Man* (New York: Boni & Liveright, 1926), 16.

"as entertaining and edifying . . ." *Monthly Magazine and American Review* 3, no. 3 (September 1800): 210.

"For very, very . . ." William A. Dunning, "Truth in History," *American Historical Review* 19, no. 2 (January 1914): 229.

Chapter One: The Flat Earth

"because the world . . ." Ferdinand Columbus, *The Life of the Admiral Christopher Columbus By His Son Ferdinand*, trans. Benjamin Keen (New Brunswick, NJ: Rutgers University Press, 1959), 39. Originally published in 1571.

"The era was distinguished . . ." "was assailed . . . ," "the expositions . . ." "To his simplest . . ." "there are any so foolish . . ." "but there was a preponderating . . ." Washington Irving, *History of the Life and Voyages of Christopher Columbus* (Philadelphia: Lea & Blanchard, 1841), 1: 51, 52, 53–54, 56.

"I have come to another conclusion . . ." "The History of a Voyage which Don Christopher Columbus made the third time that he came to the Indies, when he discovered terra firma, and which he sent to their Majesties from the Island of Hispaniola" in *Four Voyages to the New World: Letters and Selected Documents*, ed. and trans. R. H. Major (New York: Corinth Books, 1961), 130.

"I am convinced that it is the spot . . ." Ibid., 137.

"Columbia's distant fertile Plains . . ." *Boston-Gazette and Country Journal*, February 13, 1775.

"Columbus, striking it gently . . ." *The Columbian Reader; Containing a New and Choice Collection of Descriptive, Narrative, Argumentative, Pathetic, Humorous, and Entertaining Pieces, Together With Speeches, Orations, Addresses, & Harangues. To Which is Added, A New Collection of Dialogues, Designed for the Use of Schools*, 3rd ed. (Cooperstown, NY: E. Phinney, 1815), 45.

"grumbling, lamenting, and plotting" Ferdinand Columbus, *Life of the Admiral Christopher Columbus*, 53.

"the constant danger . . ." "throw him into the sea . . ." "kept a serene and steady countenance." Washington Irving. *History of the Life and Voyages*, 1: 94, 95.

"The generous spirit . . ." Ibid, 1: 71.

"nights of our intimacy" Alejo Carpentier, *The Harp and the Shadow*, trans. Thomas Christensen and Carol Christensen (San Francisco: Mercury House, 1990), 68.

"a man of great . . ." "the dissolute rabble . . ." "bigotry of the age" "was goaded on . . ." Washington Irving, *History of the Life and Voyages*, 2: 200, 201, 203.

"anthems in new tongues . . ." Walt Whitman, "Prayer of Columbus," *Harper's Monthly Magazine* 48 (March 1874): 525.

"In fourteen hundred ninety-two . . ." Winifred Sackville Stoner Jr., "The History of the U.S." *Yankee Doodles*, ed. Ted Malone (New York: Whittlesey House, 1943), 61.

"Of course I can" and "In fourteen hundred ninety three . . ." "Too Poetical," *Atchison Champion* (Atchison, KS), August 13, 1890, 5.

Chapter Two: The Indian Princess

"ready with their clubs . . ." and "Pocahontas, the king's dearest daughter . . ." John Smith, *The Generall Historie of Virginia, New-England, and the Summer Isles*, 1624 in *The Complete Works of Captain John Smith*, ed. Philip L. Barbour (Chapel Hill: University of North Carolina Press, 1986), 2: 151.

"be kept til such time . . ." Ralph Hamor, *A True Discourse of the Present Estate of Virginia . . .* (London: John Beale, 1615), 6.

"for the glory of God ..." "carnal affection," and "Christians more pleasing" Hamor, *A True Discourse*, 63, 67.

"still carried herself ..." Samuel Purchas, *Hakluytus Posthumus, or Purchas his Pilgrimes* (New York: Macmillan, 1906), 19: 117–18. Originally published in 1625.

"They did tell us always ..." Smith, *The Generall Historie*, 2: 261.

"the beauteous Lady Tragabigzanda ..." "the charitable Lady Callamata ...," and "the good Lady Madam Chanoyes ..." Smith, *The Generall Historie*, 2: 41–42.

"threw herself upon his body," "threw herself into his arms," and "wept bitterly" Marquis de Chastellux, *Travels in North America in the Years 1780, 1781 and 1782*, trans. Howard C. Rice Jr. (Chapel Hill: University of North Carolina Press, 1963), 2: 423, 424. Originally published in 1786.

"Never did the moon ..." "she gave loose ..." "possessed not the ambition ..." "Here as I pensive wander ..." "the impassioned youth ..." "The breast of a woman ..." "the broken fragment ..." John Davis, *Travels of Four Years and a Half in the United States of America During 1798, 1799, 1800, 1801, and 1802*, introduction and notes by A. J. Morrison (New York: Henry Holt and Company, 1909), 297, 303, 308, 311, 312, 321. Originally published in 1803.

"An Original Aboriginal ..." and "the beautiful ..." John Brougham, *Po-ca-hon-tas or the Gentle Savage* in *Dramas from the American Theatre, 1762–1902*, ed. Richard Moody (Cleveland: World Publishing Company, 1966), 403, 404.

"Cruel king ..." George Washington Custis, *Pocahontas; or The Settlers of Virginia* in *Representative American Plays from 1767 to the Present Day*, ed. Arthur Hobson Quinn (New York: Appleton-Century Crofts, 1938), 191.

"'tis no dream!" Charlotte M. S. Barnes, *Plays Prose and Poetry* (Philadelphia: E.H. Butler & Co.), 1848, 263.

"addresses itself ..." John Gadsby Chapman, *The Picture of the Baptism of Pocahontas* (Washington: Peter Force, 1840), 5.

"be a pledge . . ." and "a long line . . ." George Washington Custis, *Pocahontas*, 192.

"And now in the light . . ." John Esten Cooke, "A Dream of the Cavaliers" in *Harper's New Monthly Magazine* 22, no. 128 (January 1861), 253.

"remarkable for a curious air . . ." *North American Review* 214 (January 1867), 10.

"The story of one Indian . . ." Ann Uhry Abrams, *The Pilgrims and Pocahontas* (Boulder, CO: Westview Press, 1999), 165.

"Next time you pour . . ." Advertisement for Old Grand Dad Bourbon, 1987. Included in "Americans" exhibit at National Museum of American Indian, 2018–2022.

"the world's sudsiest cleanser" Advertisement for Bab-o, 1952. Included in "Pocahontas Imagined" exhibit at Jamestown Settlement, 2017–2018.

"very mad affair" Peggy Lee, "Fever," on *Peggy Lee At Her Best*, https://genius.com/Peggy-lee-fever-lyrics. The original version of the song was written by Eddie Cooley and Otis Blackwell and was first recorded by William Edward "Little Willie" John.

"Pocahontas is suddenly part . . ." Martina Whelshula and Faith Spotted Eagle, "It May Be Art But . . . It Isn't Reality," Spokane *Review-Perspective*, June 11, 1995.

"I grew up . . ." Mal Vincent, "Disney vs. History . . . Again," *The Virginian-Pilot*, June 20, 1995.

CHAPTER THREE: GIVING THANKS

"Now began to come . . ." William Bradford, *Of Plymouth Plantation 1620–1647*, ed. Samuel Eliot Morison (New York: Knopf, 1952), 90.

"whom for three days . . ." Edward Winslow, "A letter sent from New England to a friend in these parts, setting forth a brief and true declaration of the worth of that plantation; as also certain useful directions for such as intend a voyage into those parts" in *Mourt's*

Relation: A Journal of the Pilgrims of Plymouth, ed. Jordan D. Fiore. (Plymouth, MA: Plymouth Rock Foundation, 1985), 72.

"all ye Pilgrims . . ." See, for example, https://christiananswers.net/ q-eden/ednkc002.html or http://www.appleseeds.org/thankgv6. htm.

"the evil examples" and "into extravagant . . ." Bradford, *Of Plymouth*, 25.

"strangers" Ibid., 44.

"set apart a day . . ." Ibid., 132.

"the first Thanksgiving" Alexander Young, *Chronicle of the Pilgrim Fathers from 1602 to 1625* (Boston: Charles C. Little and James Brown, 1841), 231.

"Mary had a little lamb" Sarah J. Hale, *The School Song Book* (Boston: Allen & Ticknor, 1834), 14.

"as a day . . ." and "harmony has prevailed" "Proclamation of Thanksgiving, Oct. 3, 1863" in *Collected Works of Abraham Lincoln*, Roy P. Basler, ed. (New Brunswick, NJ: Rutgers University Press, 1953), 497. Franklin Roosevelt changed the holiday from the last Thursday to the fourth Thursday of November in order to satisfy retailers by extending the Christmas shopping season.

"birth of popular constitutional . . ." George Bancroft, *History of the United States from the Discovery of the American Continent* (Boston: Charles C. Little and James Brown, 1848), 1: 310.

"combine ourselves . . ." and "constitute and frame . . ." *Mourt's Relation*, 14. A nearly identical version of the Mayflower Compact appeared in Bradford's *Of Plymouth Plantation*.

"perhaps the only instance . . ." John Quincy Adams, *An Oration Delivered at Plymouth, December 22, 1802* (Boston: Russell and Cutler, 1802), 17.

"avarice and ambition" Ibid., 13.

"assent by all . . ." Ibid., 18.

"a very good harbor," and "marched also . . ." *Mourt's Relation*, 33.

"impressed his mind" and "bedewed it . . ." James Thacher, *History of the Town of Plymouth; from its first settlement in 1620, to the year 1832* (Boston: Marsh, Capen & Lyon, 1832), 30.

"the separation of the rock . . ." Ibid., 202.

"'If God prosper us . . .'" Daniel Webster, *A Discourse Delivered at Plymouth, December 22, 1820* (Boston: Wells and Lilly, 1821), 11.

"The rock underlies . . ." Wendell Phillips, "Speech at the Dinner of the Pilgrim Society, in Plymouth, December 21, 1855" in *Selections from the Works of Wendell Phillips*, ed. A. D. Hall (Boston: H.M. Caldwell Co., 1902), 49–50.

"The Pilgrims were a simple . . ." Mark Twain, "Address at the First Annual Dinner, New England Society, Philadelphia, December 22, 1881," https://www.gutenberg.org/files/3188/3188-h/3188-h. htm#link2H_4_0004.

"the point of precedence . . ." Thacher, *History of the Town of Plymouth*, 31.

"yielded his claim . . ." William S. Russell, *Guide to Plymouth, and Recollections of the Pilgrims* (Boston: George Coolidge, 1846), 181.

"John Alden, who is said . . ." Timothy Alden, *A Collection of American Epitaphs and Inscriptions, with Occasional Notes* (New York: 1814), 3:265.

"Why don't you speak . . ." Henry Wadsworth Longfellow, *The Courtship of Miles Standish and Other Poems* (Boston: Ticknor and Fields, 1859), 42.

"Over the river . . ." "Lydia Maria Child, "The New-England Boy's Song about Thanksgiving Day" in *Flowers for Children* (New York: C.S. Francis & Co., 1854), 2: 25.

"amongst other recreations . . ." *Mourt's Relation*, 72.

"Thanksgiving is no longer . . ." *New York Herald*, December 1, 1893, 3, in Michael Oriard, *Reading Football* (Chapel Hill: University of North Carolina Press, 1993), 95.

CHAPTER FOUR: THE JOLLY ROGER

"that if he did not now and then . . ." Captain Charles Johnson, *A General History of the Robberies and Murders of the Most Notorious Pirates*, ed. David Cordingly (New York: Lyons Press, 1998), 59. Originally published in 1724.

"he assumed the cognomen . . ." and "In time of action . . ." Ibid., 60.

"alive at this time . . ." Ibid., 60.

"My name was Robert Kidd . . ." "The Dying Words of Captain Robert Kidd . . ." (Boston: Nathaniel Coverly, 1810–1814), *Isaiah Thomas Broadside Ballads Project*, accessed July 3, 2019, http://www .americanantiquarian.org/thomasballads/items/show/97.

"odd humor . . ." Benjamin Franklin, "The Busy-Body—No. VIII" (March 27, 1729) in *The Works of Benjamin Franklin*, ed. Jared Sparks (Boston: Tappan & Whittemore, 1836), 2:43.

"There comes a time . . ." Mark Twain, *The Adventures of Tom Sawyer* (Hartford, CT: American Publishing Co., 1876), 191.

"became rich and great . . ." Howard Pyle, *Howard Pyle's Book of Pirates*, compiled by Merle Johnson (New York: Harper & Brothers, 1921), 128.

"nobody but himself . . ." Johnson, *General History*, 61.

"Legends tell of his murderous . . ." "History of Blackbeard Island" at https://www.fws.gov/refuge/blackbeard_island/about/history.html.

"An idea was very prevalent . . ." John F. Watson, *Annals of Philadelphia and Pennsylvania, in the Olden Times* (Philadelphia: John Pennington and Uriah Hunt, 1844), 2: 32.

"They were now closely . . ." Johnson, *General History*, 57.

"the lieutenant caused . . ." Ibid., 58.

"the skull was made . . ." Watson, *Annals of Philadelphia*, 2: 221.

"Death to Spotswood," and "The oblate spheroid . . ." Charles Harry Whedbee, *Blackbeard's Cup and Stories of the Outer Banks* (Winston-Salem, NC: John F. Blair, 1989), 31, 33.

"He knew who stood . . ." John P. Hunter, compiler, *Ghosts Amongst Us* (Williamsburg, VA: Colonial Williamsburg, 2016), 85. Colonial Williamsburg adapted this story from one told by Catherine Albertson in *In Ancient Albemarle* (Raleigh: North Carolina Society Daughters of the American Revolution, 1914, 57–60).

"You wished for . . ." Ibid, 87.

"She fought him . . ." Johnson, *General History*, 123.

"all the comfort . . ." Ibid., 131.

"that in times of action . . ." Ibid., 121.

"all noblemen . . ." W. S. Gilbert and Arthur Sullivan, *The Pirates of Penzance*, Gilbert and Sullivan Archive, https://web.archive.org/web/20120911101936/http://math.boisestate.edu/gas/pirates/definitive_pirates.pdf.

Chapter Five: The Cherry Tree

"our political father . . ." Levi Allen to George Washington, January 27, 1776. *The Papers of George Washington Digital Edition* (Charlottesville: University of Virginia Press, Rotunda, 2008).

"You are wrong . . ." James Nicholls, "Lady Henrietta Liston's Journal of Washington's 'Resignation,' Retirement, and Death" in *Pennsylvania Magazine of History and Biography* 95, no. 4 (October 1971), 516.

"He is in our textbooks . . ." Richard Brookhiser, *Founding Father* (New York: Free Press, 1996), 4.

"The Birth . . ." John Marshall, *The Life of George Washington* (Philadelphia: C.P. Wayne, 1804), 2: 1.

"The next morning . . ." and "worth more than a thousand . . ." Mason Locke Weems, *The Life of Washington* (Armonk, NY: M.E. Sharpe, 1996), 10. This edition, with an introduction by Peter S. Onuf, is a reprint of the ninth edition of Weems's *Life,* published in Philadelphia by Matthew Carey in 1809.

"as entertaining and edifying . . ." *Monthly Magazine and American Review* 3, no. 3 (September 1800), 210.

"Only those who willfully . . ." William Roscoe Thayer, *George Washington* (Boston: Houghton Mifflin Company, 1922), vii.

"When we have done wrong . . ." and "What may we expect . . ." W. H. McGuffey, *The Eclectic Second Reader* (Cincinnati: Truman and Smith, 1836), 115.

"Oh papa . . ." Morrison Heady, *The Farmer Boy, and How He Became Commander-in-Chief* (Boston: Walker, Wise, and Company, 1864), 45.

"burst his noble heart" and "I rejoice . . ." George Washington Parke Custis, *Recollections and Private Memoirs of Washington* (New York: Derby & Jackson, 1860), 133, 134.

"It is hard to believe . . ." Henry Wiencek, *An Imperfect God* (New York: Farrar, Straus and Giroux, 2003), 33.

"From his infancy . . ." George Washington to Samuel Stanhope Smith, 24 May 1797 in *The Papers of George Washington, Retirement Series*, vol. 1, *4 March 1797–30 December 1797*, ed. W. W. Abbot (Charlottesville: University Press of Virginia, 1998), 153–54.

"I profess. . ." "I feel the force . . ." and "The world has no business . . ." George Washington to Sarah Cary Fairfax, 12 September 1758, *The Papers of George Washington, Colonial Series, 4 September 1758–26 December 1760*, ed. W. W. Abbot (Charlottesville: University Press of Virginia, 1988), 6: 11.

"not even marriage . . ." Moncure D. Conway, "Footprints in Washingtonland," *Harper's New Monthly Magazine* 78, no. 467 (April 1889), 739.

"fierce passion . . ." Bernie Babcock, *Heart of George Washington: A Simple Story of Great Love* (Philadelphia: J.B. Lippincott Company, 1932).

"Early in life . . ." W. E. Woodward, *The Image and the Man* (New York: Boni and Liveright, 1926), 38.

"Whom should he behold . . ." M .L. Weems, *The Life of George Washington* (Philadelphia: R. Cochran, 1808), 183–84.

"falling to his knees . . ." "Second Inaugural Address of Ronald Reagan, January 21, 1985," http://avalon.law.yale.edu/20th_century/reagan2.asp.

"Son of the Republic . . ." Wesley Bradshaw, *Washington's Vision* (Philadelphia: C.W. Alexander & Co. 1864, 15). The story appeared in a number of newspapers before being published in this pamphlet.

"And now . . ." J. G. Bell, "The Truth of Washington's Vision," September 30, 2006 at http://boston1775.blogspot.com/2006/12/truth-of-washingtons-vision.html.

"indispensable supports" and "political prosperity" George Washington, "Farewell Address, 19 September 1796," *Founders Online*, National Archives, last modified February 1, 2018, http://founders.archives.gov/documents/Washington/99-01-02-00963.

"The image . . ." David Hackett Fischer, *Washington's Crossing* (New York: Oxford University Press, 2004), 1.

"would have made Washington hesitate . . ." Mark Twain, *Life on the Mississippi* (New York: Harper & Brothers, 1883), 279.

"hundred-dollar bill . . ." George C. Mason, *The Life and Works of Gilbert Stuart* (New York: Charles Scribner's Sons, 1879), 106.

CHAPTER SIX: BETSY ROSS'S FLAG

"Washington was a frequent visitor . . ." George Henry Preble, *History of the Flag of the United States of America* (Boston; A. Williams and Company, 1880), 266–67.

"ridiculous . . ." Ibid., 267.

"The naïve conception . . ." M. M. Quaife, *The Flag of the United States* (New York: Grosset & Dunlap, 1942), 187.

"challenged George Washington's design . . ." Laurel Thatcher Ulrich, "How Betsy Ross Became Famous." *Common-place.org* 8, no. 1 (October 2007), http://common-place.org/book/how-betsy-ross-became-famous/.

"became America's founding mother . . ." Valerie Reitman, "Tale of Betsy Ross It Seems Was Made Out of Whole Cloth," *Wall Street Journal*, June 12, 1992, in Marc Leepson, *Flag: An American Biography* (New York, Thomas Dunne Books, 2005), 43.

"While there is no real evidence . . ." Vicki Cox, *Betsy Ross: A Flag for a New Nation* (Philadelphia: Chelsea House, 2006), 10.

"Some people believe . . ." Ryan P. Randolph, *Betsy Ross: The American Flag and Life in a Young America* (New York: Rosen Publishing Group, 2002), 90.

"She is important . . ." Marla R. Miller, *Betsy Ross and the Making of America* (New York: Henry Holt, 2010), 361.

"Her story is worth knowing . . ." Ibid., 362.

CHAPTER SEVEN: MOLLY'S PITCHER

"Captain Molly" and "Her husband received . . ." George Washington Parke Custis, *Recollections and Private Memoirs of Washington* (New York: Derby & Jackson, 1860), 225.

"A woman whose husband . . ." James Kirby Martin, ed., *Ordinary Courage: The Revolutionary War Adventures of Joseph Plumb Martin* (Malden, MA: Blackwell Publishing, 2008), 89. The original edition of Martin's *Narrative of Some of the Adventures, Dangers, and Sufferings of a Revolutionary Soldier* was published in 1830.

"Oh, Molly, Molly . . ." John B. Landis, *A Short History of Molly Pitcher: The Heroine of the Battle of Monmouth* (Carlisle, PA: District of Cumberland Country Patriotic Order of Sons of America, 1905), 15. Landis doesn't name the poet; she was Laura E. Richards.

"swerved from the accustomed . . ." Elizabeth Evans, *Weathering the Storm: Women of the American Revolution* (New York: Charles Scribner's Sons, 1975), 327.

"When I heard . . ." Paul Revere to Congressman William Eustis of Massachusetts, 1804, in Evans, *Weathering the Storm*, 330.

"The career to which . . ." Elizabeth F. Ellet, *The Women of the American Revolution* (New York: Baker and Scribner), 1849, 2: 135.

"While only two . . ." Emily J. Teipe, "Will the Real Molly Pitcher Please Stand Up?" *Prologue* 31, no. 2 (Summer 1999), https://www.archives.gov/publications/prologue/1999/summer/pitcher.html.

"Pitcher, Molly, pitcher . . ." "Molly Pitcher," music and lyrics by Danny O'Flaherty and Khaetidawne Quirk.

CHAPTER EIGHT: THE MIDNIGHT RIDE

"I proceeded immediately . . ." Paul Revere, "The Deposition: Corrected Copy," in *Paul Revere's Three Accounts of His Famous Ride* (Massachusetts Historical Society, 1968).

"I told him the family . . ." Elias Phinney, *History of the Battle of Lexington on the Morning of the 19th of April 1775* (Boston: Phelps and Farnum, 1825), 33.

"had alarmed the country . . ." *Paul Revere's Three Accounts*.

"the shot heard round the world" Ralph Waldo Emerson, "Hymn: Sung at the Completion of the Concord Monument, April 19, 1837" in *Poems* by Ralph Waldo Emerson (Boston: Houghton Mifflin, 1904), 158.

"myth of injured innocence" David Hackett Fischer, *Paul Revere's Ride* (New York: Oxford University Press, 1994), 327.

"He madly dashed . . ." Quoted in Fischer, *Paul Revere's Ride*, 328.

"one of the earliest . . ." *New-England Galaxy*, May 15, 1818, 3.

"Listen my children . . ." "Paul Revere's Ride" in *Tales of a Wayside Inn* by Henry Wadsworth Longfellow (Boston: Ticknor and Fields, 1864), 18–25.

"We have heard of poetic license . . ." Charles Hudson, *History of the Town of Lexington* (Boston: Wiggin & Lunt, 1868), 171.

"a solitary hero . . ." Fischer, *Paul Revere's Ride*, 332.

"destined forever . . ." Esther Forbes, *Paul Revere and the World He Lived In* (Boston: Houghton Mifflin, 1942), 464.

"a-hollerin' at the top of his lungs . . ." "Andy Discovers America," episode of *The Andy Griffith Show*, first aired March 4, 1963.

"wandering, bitter shade" and "'Tis all very well . . ." Helen F. More, "What's in a Name" in *Century Illustrated Magazine* 51 (1896), 639.

"Come gather round . . ." The line is quoted in the Wikipedia entry for Dawes but no citation is given.

"busy with some sort . . ." Robert Benchley, "Paul Revere's Ride: How a Modest Go-Getter Did His Bit for the Juno Acid Corporation" in Robert Benchley, *The Benchley Roundup: A Selection by Nathaniel Benchley* (Chicago: University of Chicago Press, 1954), 98.

"I love the story . . ." Warren G. Harding, *Speeches and Addresses of Warren G. Harding, President of the United States, Delivered During the Course of His Tour from Washington, D.C., to Alaska and Return to San Francisco, June 20 to August 2, 1923,* reported and compiled by James W. Murphy, 1923, 256.

Chapter Nine: Poor Richard

"a natural inclination . . ." Silence Dogood, No. 2, *New-England Courant,* April 16, 1722, *Founders Online,* National Archives, last modified June 13, 2018, http://founders.archives.gov/documents/Franklin/01-01-02-0009. [Original source: *The Papers of Benjamin Franklin, January 6, 1706, through December 31, 1734,* ed.

Leonard W. Labaree. New Haven: Yale University Press, 1959, 1: 11–13.]

"Early to bed . . ." *Poor Richard, 1735, Founders Online,* National Archives, last modified June 13, 2018, http://founders.archives .gov/documents/Franklin/01-02-02-0001. [Original source: *The Papers of Benjamin Franklin,* vol. 2, *January 1, 1735, through December 31, 1744,* ed. Leonard W. Labaree. New Haven: Yale University Press, 1961, 2: 3–12.]

"Fish and visitors . . ." *Poor Richard, 1736, Founders Online,* National Archives, last modified June 13, 2018, http://founders.archives. gov/documents/Franklin/01-02-02-0019. [Original source: *The Papers of Benjamin Franklin, January 1, 1735, through December 31, 1744,* ed. Leonard W. Labaree. New Haven: Yale University Press, 1961, 2: 136–45.]

"Three may keep a secret . . ." *Poor Richard, 1735, Founders Online,* National Archives, last modified June 13, 2018, http://founders. archives.gov/documents/Franklin/01-02-02-0001. [Original source: *The Papers of Benjamin Franklin, January 1, 1735, through December 31, 1744,* ed. Leonard W. Labaree. New Haven: Yale University Press, 1961, 2: 3–12.]

"Having emerged . . ." Benjamin Franklin, *The Autobiography* (New York: Library of America, 1990), 3. Originally published in France in 1791 and in Philadelphia in 1794.

"the counselor and household friend . . ." Nathaniel Hawthorne, *Tales, Sketches, and Other Papers* (Boston: Houghton Mifflin, 1850, 202).

"The sleeping fox . . ." *Poor Richard, 1743, Founders Online,* National Archives, last modified June 13, 2017, http://founders.archives.gov/ documents/Franklin/01-02-02-0089. [Original source: *The Papers of Benjamin Franklin,* vol. 2, *January 1, 1735, through December 31, 1744,* ed. Leonard W. Labaree. New Haven: Yale University Press, 1961, 365–74.]

"Diligence is the mother . . ." *Poor Richard, 1736, Founders Online,* National Archives, last modified June 13, 2018, http:// founders.archives.gov/documents/Franklin/01-02-02-0019. [Original source: *The Papers of Benjamin Franklin,* vol. 2, *January*

1, 1735, through December 31, 1744, ed. Leonard W. Labaree. New Haven: Yale University Press, 1961, 136–45.]

"Haste makes waste . . ." *Poor Richard Improved, 1753, Founders Online,* National Archives, last modified June 13, 2018, http://founders.archives.gov/documents/Franklin/01-04-02-0148. [Original source: *The Papers of Benjamin Franklin,* vol. 4, *July 1, 1750, through June 30, 1753,* ed. Leonard W. Labaree. New Haven: Yale University Press, 1961, 403–9.]

"No gains without pains . . ." *Poor Richard, 1745, Founders Online,* National Archives, last modified June 13, 2018, http://founders.archives.gov/documents/Franklin/01-03-02-0001. [Original source: *The Papers of Benjamin Franklin,* vol. 3, *January 1, 1745, through June 30, 1750,* ed. Leonard W. Labaree. New Haven: Yale University Press, 1961, 3–9.]

"God helps them . . ." *Poor Richard, 1736, Founders Online,* National Archives, last modified June 13, 2018, http://founders.archives.gov/documents/Franklin/01-02-02-0019. [Original source: *The Papers of Benjamin Franklin,* vol. 2, *January 1, 1735, through December 31, 1744,* ed. Leonard W. Labaree. New Haven: Yale University Press, 1961, 136–45.]

"If, like Franklin . . ." Mason Locke Weems, *The Life of Benjamin Franklin with many choice anecdotes and admirable sayings of this great man* (Philadelphia: Uriah Hunt, 1829), 49. Originally published in 1818.

"For so poor . . ." and "exactly suited . . ." Thomas Mellon, *Thomas Mellon and His Times* (Pittsburgh: University of Pittsburgh Press, 1994), 33. Originally published in 1885.

"are all about getting money . . ." and "they teach men . . ." Hawthorne, *Tales, Sketches, and Other Papers,* 202.

"jack of all trades . . ." Herman Melville, *Israel Potter* (New York: Putnam, 1855), 81.

"I know it is not so . . ." Mark Twain, *The Works of Mark Twain: Early Tales and Sketches,* ed. Edgar Marquess Branch and Robert H. Hirst (Berkeley: University of California Press, 1981), 2: 24–25.

"Most wealthy people . . ." Groucho Marx, *Groucho and Me* (Boston: Da Capo Press, 1995), 9. Originally published in 1959.

"our founding yuppie . . ." David Brooks, "Our Founding Yuppie," *Weekly Standard*, October 23, 2000.

"I would rather . . ." "Benjamin Franklin to Abiah Franklin, 12 April 1750," *Founders Online*, National Archives, last modified June 13, 2018, http://founders.archives.gov/documents/Franklin/01-03-02-0189. [Original source: *The Papers of Benjamin Franklin*, vol. 3, *January 1, 1745, through June 30, 1750*, ed. Leonard W. Labaree. New Haven: Yale University Press, 1961, 474–75.]

"Figure me . . ." Benjamin Franklin to Emma Thompson, 8 February 1777, *Founders Online*, National Archives, last modified June 13, 2018, http://founders.archives.gov/documents/Franklin/01-23-02-0188. [Original source: *The Papers of Benjamin Franklin*, vol. 23, *October 27, 1776, through April 30, 1777*, ed. William B. Willcox. New Haven and London: Yale University Press, 1983, 296–99.]

"I found that the business . . ." May 27th. Wednesday, *Diary of John Adams. Founders Online*, National Archives, last modified June 13, 2018, http://founders.archives.gov/documents/Adams/01-04-02-0001-0091. [Original source: *The Adams Papers*, Diary and Autobiography of John Adams, vol. 4, *Autobiography, Parts Two and Three, 1777–1780*, ed. L. H. Butterfield. Cambridge, MA: Harvard University Press, 1961, 118–19.]

"frequently locking her hand . . ." Abigail Adams to Lucy Cranch, 5 September 1784, *Founders Online*, National Archives, last modified June 13, 2018, http://founders.archives.gov/documents/Adams/04-05-02-0229. [Original source: *The Adams Papers*, Adams Family Correspondence, vol. 5, *October 1782–November 1784*, ed. Richard Alan Ryerson. Cambridge, MA: Harvard University Press, 1993, 436–39.]

"one of our first jacobins . . ." *Port Folio*, 1st series, 1 (February 14, 1801), 53-54 in *Benjamin Franklin's Autobiography*, edited by J. A, Leo Lemay and P. M. Zall (New York: Norton, 1986) 252.

"the homage . . ." Melville, *Israel Potter*, 81.

"As he has already given her . . ." Benjamin Franklin to Madame Helvetius, through Pierre-Jean-Georges Cabinis, September 19, 1779, in Walter Isaacson, *Benjamin Franklin* (New York: Simon & Schuster, 2003), 365.

"When I was a young man . . ." Benjamin Franklin to Madame Brillion, November 26, 1780, in Isaacson, *Benjamin Franklin*, 370.

"many masks" Gordon Wood, *The Americanization of Benjamin Franklin* (New York: Penguin Press, 2004), 13.

"many Franklins . . ." John Updike, "Many Bens," *New Yorker*, February 22, 1988, 106.

"Right here, John . . ." *1776*, scene 2. Music by Sherman Edwards, book by Peter Stone.

CHAPTER TEN: ELBOW ROOM

"elbow room . . ." Timothy Flint, *The First White Man of the West or the Life and Exploits of Col. Daniel Boone . . .* (Cincinnati: George Conclin, 1847), 238. Originally published in 1833.

"I first removed . . ." *Niles' Weekly Register* (Baltimore), May 17, 1823, 166.

"barking off squirrels . . ." John James Audubon, *Ornithological Biography, or an account of the birds of the United States of America; accompanied by descriptions of the objects represented in the book entitled The Birds of America, and interspersed with delineations of American scenery and manners* (Edinburgh: Adam Black, 1831), 293–94.

"fire hunt . . ." Flint, *First White Man of the West*, 26–29.

"It will be a Boone . . ." Stephen Hempstead to Lyman Coleman Draper, February 15, 1863, in Meredith Mason Brown, *Frontiersman* (Baton Rouge: Louisiana State University Press, 2008), 26.

"You had better . . ." Lyman Coleman Draper interview with Stephen Cooper, 1889, in Brown, *Frontiersman*, 26.

"rising from obscurity . . ." John Filson, *The Discovery, Settlement and present State of Kentucke: And an Essay towards the Topography and Natural History of that important Country: To which is added, An Appendix, Containing . . . The Adventures of Col. Daniel Boon, one of the first Settlers . . .* (Wilmington, DE: James Adams, 1784), 50.

"The sovereign law . . ." Daniel Bryan, *The Mountain Muse: Comprising the Adventures of Daniel Boone and the Power of Virtuous and Refined Beauty* (Harrisonburg, VA: Davidson & Bourne, 1813), 59.

"ought to be left . . ." Draper manuscript collection, in Michael A. Lofaro, *Daniel Boone* (Lexington: University Press of Kentucky, 2003), 168.

"Of the great names . . ." Lord Byron, *Don Juan* (Halifax, England: Milner and Sowerby, 1837). Canto 8, which includes the stanzas on Boone, was originally published in 1823.

"try yourself . . ." Brown, *Frontiersman*, 263.

"a philosopher . . ." James Fenimore Cooper, *The Prairie* (Newcastle upon Tyne, England: Cambridge Scholars Publishing, 2009), 3. *The Prairie* was originally published in 1827, but the passage quoted first appeared in an introduction to an 1851 edition.

"thrilling excitement . . ." John A. McClung, *Sketches of Western Adventure . . .* (Cincinnati: U.P. James, 1839), 79. Originally published in 1832.

"was made not for use . . ." Quoted in John Mack Faragher, *Daniel Boone* (New York: Henry Holt, 1992), 323.

"On the fourteenth . . ." Filson, *Discovery, Settlement and present State of Kentucke*, 60.

"leaped from his bed . . ." Lyman C. Draper, *The Life of Daniel Boone*, ed. Ted Franklin Belue (Mechanicsburg, PA: Stackpole Books, 1988, 416, 419). Draper stopped work on his unfinished biography in 1856.

"killed a host . . ." Draper manuscript collection, in Brown, *Frontiersman*, 2.

"the rich and boundless . . ." Flint, *First White Man of the West*, 226–27.

"an American Moses . . ." J. Gray Sweeney, *The Columbus of the Woods* (St. Louis: Washington University Gallery of Art, 1992), 41.

"an instrument ordained . . ." Filson, *Discovery, Settlement and present State of Kentucke*, 81.

"I think we took . . ." "The Choosing," episode from season 1 of *Daniel Boone*, originally aired October 29, 1964.

-Tuck-E,” episode from season 1 of *Daniel
  Boone*, originally aired September 24, 1964.

CHAPTER ELEVEN: THE INDIAN GUIDE

"When the white captains . . ." George Creel, "Path of Empire," *Collier's*, April 17, 1926, 7–8, in W. Dale Nelson, *Interpreters with
  Lewis and Clark: The Story of Sacagawea and Toussaint Charbonneau*
  (Denton: University of North Texas Press, 2003), 10.

"interpretess . . ." William Clark, July 3, 1806, *The Lewis and Clark
  Journals: An American Epic of Discovery*, ed. Gary E. Moulton (Lincoln: University of Nebraska Press, 2003), 353. This is an abridged
  version of the Nebraska edition of the journals.

"great service to me . . ." William Clark, July 13, 1806. Ibid., 355.

"Americans have never . . ." Richard White, "Frederick Jackson Turner
  and Buffalo Bill," *The Frontier in American Culture*, ed. James B.
  Grossman (Berkeley: University of California Press, 1994), 7.

"Madonna of her race . . ." Eva Emery Dye, *The Conquest: The True Story
  of Lewis and Clark* (New York: Wilson-Erickson, 1936), 290.

"was a princess . . ." Ibid., 228.

"there is nothing in the least . . ." Donald Culross Peattie, *Forward the
  Nation* (New York: G.P. Putnam's Sons, 1942), Foreword (unpaginated).

"as pure and clear . . ." Ibid., 233.

"Janey . . ." and "Pomp . . ." William Clark to Toussaint Charbonneau,
  August 20, 1806, in *Letters of the Lewis and Clark Expedition
  with Related Documents 1783–1854*, ed. Donald Jackson (Urbana:
  University of Illinois Press, 1962), 1: 315. Jackson notes that it is
  tempting to suppose that Clark may have written "Jawey," which
  would be a more understandable nickname for someone whose
  name was sometimes spelled Sacajawea, but the original was
  clearly Janey.

"Chief Red Head" and "her heart pounding . . ." Della Gould Emmons,
  Sacajawea of the Shoshones (Portland, OR: Binfords & Mort, 1943),
  134.

"Of course this little woman . . ." Ibid., 135.

"alight with the worship . . ." Ibid., 106.

"This feeling had roots . . ." Anna Lee Waldo, *Sacajawea* (New York: Avon, 1980), 664. Originally published in 1978.

"She had not come this distance . . ." Ibid., 569.

"This recognition . . ." Ida Husted Harper, *The Life and Work of Susan B. Anthony* (Indianapolis: Hollenbeck Press, 1908), 3: 1365 in *Lewis & Clark: Legacies, Memories, and New Perspectives,* eds. Kris Fresonke and Mark Spence (Berkeley: University of California Press, 2004), 185.

"We don't want . . ." Darrell Robes Kipp, filmed interview by Sally Thompson, July 30, 2005, in Frederick E. Hoxie and Jay T. Nelson, *Lewis and Clark and the Indian Country: The Native American Perspective* (Urbana: University of Illinois Press, 2007), 332–33.

CHAPTER TWELVE: KING OF THE WILD FRONTIER

"I never ran away . . ." and "whisky can't make me drunk . . ." *Missouri Republican*, August 15, 1829, in Michael Wallis, *David Crockett* (New York: W.W. Norton & Co., 2011), 215.

"whip his weight . . ." *Adams Sentinel* (Gettysburg, PA), December 17, 1828, in Wallis, *David Crockett*, 234.

"I'm half horse . . ." James Kirke Paulding, *The Lion of the West*, ed. James N. Tidwell (Stanford, CA: Stanford University Press, 1954), 21.

"I discovered . . ." James Strange French, *The Life and Adventures of Colonel David Crockett of West Tennessee* (Cincinnati: E. Deming, 1833), 115. Some Crockett scholars, notably James Shackford, have argued that the author was not French but Matthew St. Claire Clarke.

"I got along . . ." David Crockett, *A Narrative of the Life of David Crockett of the State of Tennessee* (Philadelphia: E.L. Cary and A. Hart, 1834), 190.

"I went to a tree . . ." Ibid., 191.

"I knowed . . ." Ibid., 169.

"I leave this rule . . ." Ibid., title page.

"I told the voters . . ." James D. Davis, *History of Memphis* (Memphis: Hite, Crumpton & Kelly, 1873), 143.

"died without complaining . . ." José Enrique de la Peña, *With Santa Anna in Texas: A Personal Narrative of the Revolution*, trans. Carmen Perry (College Station: Texas A&M University Press, 1975), 53.

"Pop, pop, pop! . . ." David Crockett, *Colonel Crockett's Exploits and Adventures in Texas* (Philadelphia: T.K. and P.G. Collins, 1836). 202. The actual writer was Richard Penn Smith.

"axletrissity . . ." "The Colonel Swallows a Thunderbolt," in Richard M. Dorson, ed. *Davy Crockett: American Comic Legend* (New York: Spiral Press, 1939), 9–10.

"So, in order to remove . . ." "Drinking Up the Gulf of Mexico" in Dorson, *Davy Crockett*, 158.

"I war out in the forest . . ." "A Sensible Varmint" in Dorson, *Davy Crockett*, 111–12.

"I can walk like an ox . . ." *Davy Crockett's 1837 Almanack of Wild Sports in the West, Life in the Backwoods & Sketches of Texas*, in Mark Derr, *The Frontiersman* (New York: William Morrow, 1993), 258.

"chased a crockodile . . ." "The Flower of Gum Swamp," in Dorson, *Davy Crockett*, 47.

"stamped them to death . . ." "Colonel Coon's Wife Judy," in Dorson, *Davy Crockett*, 49.

"fought a duel once . . ." "Sal Fink, the Mississippi Screamer," in Dorson, *Davy Crockett*, 49.

"a gal that . . ." "Crockett Popping the Question," in Dorson, *Davy Crockett*, 56.

CHAPTER THIRTEEN: APPLE SEEDS

"When the settlers . . ." "A Leaf in the History of Pomology at the West," *Magazine of Horticulture, Botany, and All Useful Discoveries in Rural Affairs*, ed. C. M. Hovey, 12 (April 1846), 134.

"He visited every cabin . . ." W. D. Haley, "Johnny Appleseed," *Harper's New Monthly Magazine*, November 1871, 833.

"the oddest . . ." A. Banning Norton, *A History of Knox County, Ohio* (Columbus: Richard Nevins, 1862), 50.

"Generally, even in the coldest . . ." Haley, "Johnny Appleseed," 831–32.

"a cross between . . ." William E. Leuchtenberg, "John Chapman (Johnny Appleseed)" in *Forgotten Heroes*, ed. Susan Ware (New York: Free Press, 1998), 12.

"Poor fellow . . ." Haley, "Johnny Appleseed," 834.

"when Johnny, who always camped out . . ." Ibid., 835.

"John Appleseed . . ." William Schlatter to the Reverend N. Holley, November 18, 1822, in Robert Price, *Johnny Appleseed* (Bloomington: Indiana University Press, 1954), 131.

"carnal vanities . . ." and "'Where now . . ." Haley, "Johnny Appleseed," 835.

"Johnny Appleseed was no Christian saint . . ." Michael Pollan, *The Botany of Desire* (New York: Random House, 2001), 36.

"In cities . . ." Lydia Maria Child, "Apple-seed John," in *St. Nicholas: Scribner's Illustrated Magazine for Girls and Boys* 7, no. 8 (June 1880), 605.

"at last the white man . . ." Vachel Lindsay, "Johnny Appleseed's Old Age" in Lindsay, *Collected Poems* (New York: Macmillan, 1925), 88.

"as a good apple tree . . ." Rosemary and Stephen Vincent Benét, *Johnny Appleseed* (New York: Margaret K. McElderry Books, 2001), unpaged. The poem was originally published in 1933.

"seed by seed . . ." Esmé Raji Codell, *Seed by Seed* (New York: Greenwillow Books, 2012), unpaged.

Chapter Fourteen: Abner Doubleday's Game

"made a plan . . ." Akron (OH) *Beacon Journal*, April 4, 1905, https://ourgame.mlblogs.com/the-letters-of-abner-graves-8fc6a4694419.

"is the exponent . . ." Albert G. Spalding, *America's National Game* (Lincoln: University of Nebraska Press, 1992), 4. Originally published in 1911.

"Our British cricketer . . ." Ibid., 7.

"First, that 'Base Ball' . . ." A. G. Mills to James E. Sullivan, December 30, 1907, in John Thorn, *Baseball in the Garden of Eden: The Secret History of the Early Game* (New York: Simon & Schuster, 2011), 16. The letter was originally published in the 1908 *Spalding Guide* under the heading "Final Decision of the Special Base Ball Commission."

"a masterly piece . . ." Henry Chadwick to A. G. Mills, March 20, 1908, in Thorn, *Baseball in the Garden of Eden*, 17.

"Tell the gentlemen . . ." Spalding, *America's National Game*, 361.

"Cooperstown can better . . ." Alan Taylor, *William Cooper's Town* (New York: Knopf, 1995), 384.

"the honor of . . ." Spalding, *America's National Game*, 51–52.

"fitting . . ." *The Otsego Farmer*, April 28, 1939, in James A. Vlasich, *A Legend for the Legendary: The Origin of the Baseball Hall of Fame* (Bowling Green, OH: Bowling Green State University Popular Press, 1990), 175.

"the myth has become . . ." https://baseballhall.org/about-the-hall.

"Creation myths . . ." Stephen Jay Gould, *Triumph and Tragedy in Mudville: A Lifelong Passion for Baseball* (New York: W.W. Norton, 2003), 203, 204.

Chapter Fifteen: Ain't I a Woman?

"The leaders of the movement . . ." Nell Irvin Painter, ed., *Narrative of Sojourner Truth; A Bondswoman of Olden Time, with a History of Labors and Correspondence* (New York: Penguin, 1998), 90–93. The Penguin edition is based on the 1884 edition of the *Narrative*.

"I am a woman's rights . . ." Salem *Anti-Slavery Bugle*, June 21, 1851, in Erlene Stetson and Linda David, *Glorying in Tribulation: The Life-work of Sojourner Truth* (East Lansing: Michigan State University Press, 1994), 114.

"She said she was a woman . . ." New York *Tribune*, June 6, 1851, in Stetson and David, *Glorying in Tribulation*, 114.

"the marvelous wisdom . . ." Elizabeth Cady Stanton, "Sojourner Truth on the Press," in *History of Woman Suffrage*, Elizabeth Cady Stanton, Susan B. Anthony, and Matilda Joslyn Gage, eds. (Rochester, NY: Susan B. Anthony, 1881), 2: 926.

"You know, children . . ." Ibid.

"My name was Isabella . . ." *Narrative*, 111. Stowe's article first appeared in the April 1863 issue of the *Atlantic Monthly*.

"Douglass had been describing . . ." Ibid., 114.

"a high pitch . . ." *Pennsylvania Freeman*, September 4, 1852, in Stetson and David, *Glorying in Tribulation*, 132.

"Speaking at an anti-slavery . . ." Frederick Douglass, *Life and Times of Frederick Douglass, Written by Himself* . . . (Boston: De Wolfe and Fiske, 1892), 342–43.

"not quite correct . . ." *The Commonwealth*, July 3, 1861 in Stetson and David, *Glorying in Tribulation*, 29.

"kindness and cordiality . . ." *Narrative*, 121.

"If the people . . ." Ibid., 120, 121.

"aunty, as he would his washerwoman . . ." and "I wouldn't free" Lucy N. Colman, *Reminiscences* (Buffalo, H.L. Green, 1891), 67.

"I had heard of you . . ." *Narrative*, 120

"From the head . . ." Ibid., 122.

"the first sit-in . . ." Marie Harlowe, "Sojourner Truth: The First Sit-In," *Negro History Bulletin* 29, no. 8 (Fall 1966), 173.

CHAPTER 16: THE LOG CABIN

"Now he belongs . . ." John George Nicolay and John Hay, *Abraham Lincoln: A History* (New York: The Century Co., 1890), 10: 302.

"Jesus Christ died . . ." Lloyd Lewis, *Myths After Lincoln* (New York: Harcourt, Brace, 1929), 110.

"fearful trip . . ." Walt Whitman, "O Captain! My Captain!" in Walt Whitman, *Leaves of Grass* (New York: Library of America), 1992.

"the tree which rose . . ." Gilbert Holland, *The Life of Abraham Lincoln* (Springfield, MA: Gurdon Bill, 1866), 2.

"emancipator of a race . . ." Ibid., 544.

"The story of the assassination . . ." Bocardo Bramantip, *The Abraham Lincoln Myth* (New York: Mascot Publishing Company, 1894), 15–16.

"I can contribute . . ." "The Editor's Drawer," *Harper's New Monthly Magazine* 32 (March 1866), 535.

"I have always felt . . ." *Success Magazine*, February 1904, in *Abe Lincoln Laughing*, ed. by P. M. Zall (Berkeley: University of California Press, 1982), 31. Zall traces the earliest version of this quote to an 1863 collection, *Old Abe's Joker, or Wit at the White House*.

"You can fool . . ." From a speech of Richard Price Morgan, Pontiac, IL, February 12, 1909, in Zall, *Abe Lincoln Laughing*, 139. Zall notes that Morgan claims to have heard Lincoln speak these words in 1856 but that there's no contemporary account of the oft-quoted line.

"Does this dress . . ." https://www.youtube.com/watch?v=RPX2c-QP8uoI.

"I never, ever . . ." https://www.imdb.com/title/tt0443272/trivia?ref_=tt_ql_2.

"the most attractive . . ." William H. Herndon and Jesse W. Weik, *Herndon's Lincoln*, ed. Douglas L. Wilson and Rodney O. Davis (Urbana: University of Illinois Press, 2006), 93. Originally published in 1889.

"My heart lies . . ." Ibid., 91.

"rudely torn . . ." Ibid., 96.

"He was twenty-six . . ." Carl Sandburg, *Abraham Lincoln: The Prairie Years* (New York: Charles Scribner's Sons, 1945), 1: 186. Originally published in 1926.

"it was said . . ." Carl Sandburg, Ibid., 1: 190.

"Go on Abe . . ." *Young Mr. Lincoln*, written by Lamar Trotti, directed by John Ford, 1939.

"to save his honor . . ." "years of self-torture . . . ," and "In him she saw . . ." Herndon and Weik, *Herndon's Lincoln*, 145.

"It is only the greatest . . ." Mary Raymond Shipman Andrews, "The Perfect Tribute," *Scribner's Magazine* 40 (July 1906), 24.

"We can never . . ." Thomas Dixon Jr., *The Clansman* (New York: Doubleday, Page, 1905), 47.

"Lincoln had his choice . . ." Carl Sandburg, *Abraham Lincoln: The War Years* (New York: Charles Scribner's Sons, 1939), 6: 217–18. The words of Lincoln that Sandburg quoted came from his Second Inaugural Address.

"vast moral evil . . ." Abraham Lincoln, "Speech at Chicago," July 10, 1858, in *Collected Works of Abraham Lincoln*, Roy Basler, ed. (New Brunswick, NJ: Rutgers University Press, 1953), 2: 494.

"If slavery is not wrong . . ." Abraham Lincoln to Albert Hodges, April 4, 1864, *Collected Works of Lincoln*, 7:282.

"Viewed from the genuine . . ." Frederick Douglass, *Life and Times of Frederick Douglass, Written By Himself* (Boston: De Wolfe & Fiske, 1892), 593–94.

"He was interested . . ." Robert Penn Warren interview with Malcolm X, June 2, 1964, http://malcolmxfiles.blogspot.com/2013/07/robert-penn-warren-interviews-malcolm-x.html.

"symbolic birth cabin" https://www.nps.gov/abli/index.htm.

CHAPTER SEVENTEEN: THE LOST CAUSE

"The war did not decide . . ." Edward Alfred Pollard, *The Lost Cause: A New Southern History of the War of the Confederates* (New York: E.B. Treat & Co., 1866), 752.

"elevated the African . . ." Ibid., 49.

"refined and sentimental . . ." and "coarse and materialistic . . ." Ibid., 51

"Under the sod . . ." "The Blue and the Gray," *Atlantic Monthly* 20, no. 119 (September 1867), 369.

"No time could be fitter . . ." "Battles and Leaders of the Civil War," *Century Magazine* 28 (October 1884), 943.

"had not been conquered . . ." Early's 1872 speech is in J. William Jones, *Personal Reminiscences, Anecdotes and Letters of Gen. Robert E. Lee* (New York: D. Appleton and Co., 1875), 43.

"in every part . . ." *New York Times*, May 30, 1890, 2.

"It is not expected . . ." "Patriotic School Histories," *The Confederate Veteran V* (September 1897), 450.

"Dem wuz . . ." Thomas Nelson Page, "Marse Chan," *Century Magazine* 37, no. 6 (April 1884), 935.

"T ain't needer . . ." Joel Chandler Harris, *Tales of the Home Folks in Peace and War* (Boston: Houghton Mifflin, 1898), 179.

"Civil Wargasm . . ." Tony Horwitz, *Confederates in the Attic* (New York: Vintage Books, 1998), 210.

"I admit that the South . . ." Frederick Douglass, "There Was a Right Side in the Late War," May 30, 1878, in *Selected Speeches and*

Writings, ed. Philip S. Foner (Chicago: Lawrence Hill Books, 1999), 631.

"sacred to the memory . . ." W. E. B. Du Bois, "Postscript," *The Crisis*, August 1931, 279.

Chapter Eighteen: The Noble Outlaw

"Missouri leads . . ." *Lexington Weekly Caucasian*, August 30, 1873.

"We called him an outlaw . . ." *Sedalia Democrat*, April 13, 1882 in T. J. Stiles, *Jesse James: Last Rebel of the Civil War* (New York: Knopf, 2003), 378.

"In all the history . . ." *Weekly Caucasian*, September 5, 1874.

"The blue eyes . . ." *St. Louis Dispatch*, February 10, 1874, in William A. Settle Jr., *Jesse James Was His Name* (Columbia: University of Missouri Press, 1966), 55.

"fought under . . ." *Kansas City Times* in the *Liberty Tribune*, June 24, 1870.

"one of those exhibitions . . ." *Kansas City Times*, September 25, 1872, in Stiles, *Jesse James*, 223.

"These men sometimes rob . . ." "The Chivalry of Crime," *Kansas City Times*, September 29, 1872, in Stiles, *Jesse James*, 224.

"We rob the rich . . ." *Kansas City Times*, October 15, 1872, in Stiles, *Jesse James*, 225.

"the worst man . . ." *Richmond* (MO) *Democrat*, November 20, 1879.

"James was not . . ." Stiles, *Jesse James*, 5–6.

"is about as pointless . . ." http://www.tjstiles.net/bio.htm.

"in popular culture . . ." Richard White, "Outlaw Gangs of the Middle Border: American Social Bandits, *Western Historical Quarterly* 12, no. 4 (October 1981), 387.

Chapter Nineteen: Steel-Driving Man

"steel-driving man . . ." Louis W. Chappell, *John Henry: A Folk-Lore Study* (Port Washington, NY: Kennikat Press, 1933), 103. Chappell collected many early versions of the ballad.

"is going to be the death of me . . ." Ibid.

"A man . . ." Ibid., 104.

"mountain of negative evidence . . ." Guy Johnson, *John Henry: Tracking Down a Negro Legend* (Chapel Hill: University of North Carolina Press, 1929), 53.

"If I could drive steel . . ." E. C. Perrow, "Songs and Rhymes from the South," *Journal of American Folklore* 26, no. 100 (April-June 1913), 163.

"This old hammer . . ." Chappell, *John Henry*, 99.

"John Henry was appropriated . . ." Scott Reynolds Nelson, *Steel Drivin' Man: John Henry, The Untold Story of an American Legend* (New York: Oxford University Press, 2006), 40.

"When the women . . ." Ibid., 116.

"men are always . . ." Alan Lomax, *The Folk Songs of North America in the English Language* (Garden City, NY, 1960), 553.

"John Henry had a lovin' . . ." Chappell, *John Henry*, 111.

"is amply qualified . . ." Roark Bradford, *John Henry* (New York: Literary Guild, 1931), author biography.

"You mix it up . . ." Colson Whitehead, *John Henry Days* (New York: Doubleday, 2001), 373.

"They took John Henry . . ." Nelson, *Steel Drivin' Man*, 37.

"transferred . . ." Ibid., 39. Nelson located the prison register in the Library of Virginia in Richmond.

Chapter Twenty: The Wild West

"Central casting . . ." Deanne Stillman, *Blood Brothers: The Story of the Strange Friendship between Sitting Bull and Buffalo Bill* (New York: Simon & Schuster, 2017), 143.

"We gave him three cheers . . ." William F. Cody, *The Life of Hon. William F. Cody, Known as Buffalo Bill*, ed. Frank Christianson (Lincoln: University of Nebraska Press, 2011), 351. Originally published in 1879.

"He may not really . . ." Larry McMurtry, *The Colonel and Little Missie: Buffalo Bill, Annie Oakley, and the Beginnings of Superstardom in America* (New York: Simon & Schuster, 2006), 77.

"Life is too short . . ." and "I am sorry to have lied . . ." Helen Cody Wetmore and Zane Grey, *Buffalo Bill: Last of the Great Scouts*

(Lincoln: University of Nebraska Press, 2003), 165. Originally published in 1899.

"In this way . . ." and "We would kill them off . . ." Cody, *Life of Hon. William F. Cody*, 382.

"Such a combination . . ." *Chicago Times*, December 18, 1872, in Sandra K. Sagala, *Buffalo Bill on Stage* (Albuquerque: University of New Mexico Press, 2008), 24.

"if you want to fight" and "My usual luck . . ." Cody, *Life of Hon. William F. Cody*, 403.

"The first scalp . . ." Ibid., 405.

"duel . . ." Wetmore and Grey, *Buffalo Bill*, 161.

"Foes in '76 . . ." The photograph was taken by William Notman in Montreal in 1885.

"Up to our own day . . ." Frederick Jackson Turner, "The Significance of the Frontier in American History" in Turner, *The Frontier in American History* (New York: Henry Holt, 1920), 1. The paper was originally read at a meeting of the American Historical Society, July 12, 1893.

"four centuries . . ." Turner, *Frontier in American History*, 38.

Final Thoughts

"instead of trying . . ." Frances Fitzgerald, *America Revised: History Schoolbooks in the Twentieth Century* (Boston: Atlantic Monthly Press, 1979), 49.

"the freedmen were not . . ." William Archibald Dunning, *Reconstruction Political and Economic, 1865–1867.* (New York: Harper & Brothers, 1907), 58.

"the paranoid style . . ." Richard Hofstadter, *The Paranoid Style in American Politics and Other Essays* (New York: Knopf, 1965), 3. A shorter version of the essay in this book appeared in the November 1964 issue of *Harper's Magazine*.

"Being American means . . ." Kurt Andersen, *Fantasyland: How America Went Haywire* (New York: Random House, 2017), 7.

"The result . . ." Ibid., 11.

"wishtories . . ." Stephen Aron, "The We in West," *Western Historical Quarterly* 49 (Spring 2018): 8.

Further Reading

Preface

Michael Kammen explored how Americans have viewed their past in a number of influential scholarly works, including *A Season of Youth: The American Revolution and the Historical Imagination* (Knopf, 1978) and *Mystic Chords of Memory: The Transformation of Tradition in American Culture* (Knopf, 1991).

Dixon Wecter's *The Hero in America: A Chronicle of Hero Worship* (Charles Scribner's Sons, 1941) was written as World War II approached, partly to contrast Americans' sensible attitudes toward hero-worship with the dangerous worship of Hitler, Stalin, and Mussolini. It remains nonetheless a useful and entertaining guide to Americans' changing tastes.

Ray Raphael's *Founding Myths: Stories That Hide Our Patriotic Past* (New Press, 2004) shows how many of our best-known stories obscure the democratic nature of the American Revolution.

Richard Slotkin's trilogy—*Regeneration through Violence: The Mythology of the American Frontier 1600–1860* (Wesleyan University Press, 1973), *The Fatal Environment: The Myth of the Frontier in the Age of Industrialization, 1800–1890* (Atheneum, 1985), and *Gunfighter Nation: The Myth of the Frontier in Twentieth-Century America* (Atheneum, 1992) follows the myth of the frontier from the seventeenth through the twentieth century.

Frances Fitzgerald's *America Revised: History Schoolbooks in the Twentieth Century* (Atlantic Monthly Press, 1979) and James Loewen's *Lies My Teacher Told Me: Everything Your American History Textbook Got Wrong* (New Press, 1995) chronicle myth-making in history textbooks.

Popular debunking books include Richard Shenkman's *Legends, Lies and Cherished Myths of American History* (William Morrow, 1988) and *"I Love Paul Revere, Whether He Rode or Not."* (Harper Collins, 1991).

CHAPTER ONE: THE FLAT EARTH
Of books that chronicle how Columbus was mythologized and otherwise interpreted through the ages, John Noble Wilford's *The Mysterious History of Columbus: An Exploration of the Man, the Myth, the Legacy* (Knopf, 1991) is especially absorbing and useful; Kirkpatrick Sale's *The Conquest of Paradise: Christopher Columbus and the Columbian Legacy* (Knopf, 1990) is lively and provocative, even if you don't buy Sale's argument that Columbus embodies everything wrong with America; and Claudia Bushman's *America Discovers Columbus: How an Italian Explorer Became an American Hero* (University Press of New England, 1992) focuses on the period between the American Revolution and the four hundredth anniversary of the landing. Jeffrey Burton's *Inventing the Flat Earth: Columbus and Modern Historians* (Praeger, 1991) focuses on the origins and persistence of the myth that Columbus's opponents thought the world was flat.

The best recent biography is Laurence Bergreen's *Columbus: The Four Voyages* (Viking, 2011), which persuasively portrays him as a visionary, albeit one increasingly detached from reality. Samuel Eliot Morison was a master of maritime history; like all of Morison's work, his *Admiral of the Ocean Sea: A Life of Christopher Columbus* (Little, Brown, 1942) remains a pleasure to read. So does Washington Irving's—shall we say colorful?—*Life and Voyages of Christopher Columbus* (Lea & Blanchard, 1841, originally published in 1828).

CHAPTER TWO: THE INDIAN PRINCESS
Ann Uhry Abrams's *The Pilgrims and Pocahontas: Rival Myths of American Origin* (Westview Press, 1999) and Robert S. Tilton's *Pocahontas: The Evolution of an American Narrative* (Cambridge University Press, 1994) both trace the changing views of Pocahontas. This chapter is indebted to both. For Pocahontas's evolution in children's books of the nineteenth century, see Laura Wasowicz's "The Children of Pocahontas" (*Proceedings of the American Antiquarian Society*, 1995, 377–415).

The definitive history of Jamestown is James Horn's *A Land As God Made It: Jamestown and the Birth of America* (Basic Books, 2005). Benjamin Wooley's *Savage Kingdom: The True Story of Jamestown, 1607, and the Settlement of America* (HarperCollins, 2007) and David Price's *Love and Hate in Jamestown: John Smith, Pocahontas, and the Start of a New Nation* (Knopf, 2003) offer entertaining variations.

Philip L. Barbour's *The Complete Works of Captain John Smith* (University of North Carolina Press, 1988) is still the source if you want to decide for yourself whether to believe Smith.

Camilla Townsend's *Pocahontas and the Powhatan Dilemma* (Hill and Wang, 2004) tries with considerable success to see through the Englishmen's words to the Indian woman's thoughts. Paula Gunn Allen's *Pocahontas: Medicine Woman, Spy, Entrepreneur, Diplomat* (HarperSanFrancisco, 2003) looks at her story through the lens of and in the style of Native American storytelling traditions. Frances Mossiker's *Pocahontas: The Life and the Legend* (Knopf, 1976) remains a useful biography.

CHAPTER THREE: GIVING THANKS

Ann Uhry Abrams's *The Pilgrims and Pocahontas* (Westview Press, 1999) traces the evolution of Pilgrim stories and the rivalry between the New England and Virginia myths of American origins. John Seelye's *Memory's Nation: The Place of Plymouth Rock* (University of North Carolina Press, 1998) is an exhaustive study of how the Rock has cropped up in images and words throughout history.

Popular histories of the Pilgrims include Nathan Philbrick's *Mayflower: A Story of Courage, Community, and War* (Viking, 2006), which concentrates on their history in America through King Philip's War, and Nick Bunker's *Making Haste from Babylon: The Mayflower Pilgrims and Their World* (Knopf, 2010), which illuminates their earlier history in England. Godfrey Hodgson's *A Great & Godly Adventure: The Pilgrims and the Myth of the First Thanksgiving* (Public Affairs, 2006) is also entertaining.

In *The Times of Their Lives: Life, Love, and Death in Plymouth Colony* (W. H. Freeman, 2000), James Deetz and Patricia Scott Deetz examine Plymouth from the perspectives of, respectively, an archaeologist and anthropologist, and a cultural historian.

The two most important primary sources are William Bradford's *Of Plymouth Plantation 1620–1647*, as edited by Samuel Eliot Morison (Knopf, 1952), and *Mourt's Relation: A Journal of the Pilgrims of Plymouth*, as edited by Jordan D. Fiore (Plymouth Rock Foundation, 1985). *Mourt's Relation* is generally used as the title of the booklet printed in England in 1622 and written by William Bradford and Edward Winslow. The full title of the booklet was *A Relation or Journal of the Beginnings and Proceedings of the English Plantation Settled at Plymouth in New England, by Certain English Adventurers Both Merchants and Others*. The introduction was signed by G. Mourt; hence *Mourt's Relation*.

CHAPTER FOUR: THE JOLLY ROGER
David Cordingly's *Under the Black Flag: The Romance and the Reality of Life Among the Pirates* (Random House, 1996) is an informative and entertaining survey of pirates in fact and fiction. Willard Bonner's *Pirate Laureate: The Life and Legends of Captain Kidd* (Rutgers University Press, 1947) traces the legend from sailors' ballads to the works of Irving, Cooper, Poe, and Stevenson.

Cordingly provided an introduction and commentary for an edition of Captain Charles Johnson's *A General History of the Robberies and Murders of the Most Notorious Pirates* (Lyons Press, 1988). Johnson's identity has been a subject of much debate among literary historians. For a long time many believed Johnson was Daniel Defoe, the author of *Robinson Crusoe*. That theory was largely discredited in 1988 by two Defoe scholars, P. N. Furbank and W. R. Owens.

For the lives of actual and not mythical pirates, fine biographies include Angus Konstam's *Blackbeard: America's Most Notorious Pirate* (Wiley, 2006) and Robert C. Ritchie's *Captain Kidd and the War Against the Pirates* (Harvard University Press, 1986).

CHAPTER FIVE: THE CHERRY TREE
This chapter is much indebted to Edward G. Lengel's *Inventing George Washington: America's Founder, in Myth and Memory* (HarperCollins, 2011), a thorough and entertaining study. Karal Ann Marling's *George Washington Slept Here: Colonial Revivals and American Culture, 1876–*

1986 (Harvard University Press, 1988) traces Washington imagery. Paul K. Longmore's *The Invention of George Washington* (University of California Press, 1988) stresses Washington's own role in myth-making. Garry Wills's *Cincinnatus: George Washington and the Enlightenment* (Doubleday, 1984) also looks at Washington's own image of himself, as well as that of early biographers, writers, and artists.

Ron Chernow's *Washington: A Life* (Penguin Press, 2010) is the latest one-volume biography, though with the breadth and depth of multiple volumes. Less comprehensive but well worth reading for the authors' insights and style are Joseph Ellis's *His Excellency: George Washington* (Knopf, 2004) and Richard Brookhiser's *Founding Father: Rediscovering George Washington* (Free Press, 1996).

CHAPTER SIX: BETSY ROSS'S FLAG

Marc Leepson's *Flag: An American Biography* (Thomas Dunne Books, 2005) entertainingly presents not only Ross's story but also those of others like Francis Scott Key, who wrote the words to "The Star-Spangled Banner," and Mary Pickersgill, who made the flag that inspired Key.

Marla Miller's *Betsy Ross and the Making of America* (Henry Holt, 2010) makes a compelling case that, even if the legend is untrue, Ross's life is well worth remembering.

For more general studies of women during the Revolution, see Mary Beth Norton's *Liberty's Daughters: The Revolutionary Experience of American Women, 1750–1800* (Little, Brown, 1980), Linda K. Kerber's *Women of the Republic: Intellect and Ideology in Revolutionary America* (The Institute of Early American History and Culture, 1980), Carol Berkin's *Revolutionary Mothers: Women in the Struggle for America's Independence* (Knopf, 2005), and Cokie Roberts's *Founding Mothers: The Women Who Raised Our Nation* (Harper, 2005).

CHAPTER SEVEN: MOLLY'S PITCHER

In "Will the Real Molly Pitcher Please Stand Up?" Emily J. Teipe provides concise answers to her question. The article appeared in the Summer 1999 issue of *Prologue*, the magazine of the National Archives. Ray Raphael summarizes new scholarship on the role in the Revolution of women (and also working people, soldiers, loyalists, Native Americans, and African Americans) in *A People's History of the American Revolution: How Common People Shaped the Fight for Independence* (New Press, 2001) and on Molly Pitcher in *Founding Myths* (New Press, 2004).

The closest we can come to Sampson's own account is Herman Mann's *The Female Review, or Memoirs of an American young lady whose life and character are peculiarly distinguished* (Printed for the author by Nathaniel and Benjamin Heaton, 1797). Elizabeth Evans's *Weathering the Storm: Women of the American Revolution* (Scribner's, 1975) tells Sampson's story and includes documents pertaining to it. Alfred F. Young's *Masquerade: The Life and Times of Deborah Sampson, Continental Soldier* (Knopf, 2004) probes how and why Sampson pulled off her masquerade.

In addition to the general histories of women in the Revolution listed under "Further Reading" on Betsy Ross, works by Linda Grant De Pauw offer some additional focus on women and the military. These include *Battle Cries and Lullabies: Women in War from Prehistory to the Present* (University of Oklahoma Press, 1998), and *Founding Mothers: Women of America in the Revolutionary Era* (Houghton Mifflin, 1975).

CHAPTER EIGHT: THE MIDNIGHT RIDE

This chapter is greatly indebted to David Hackett Fischer's authoritative *Paul Revere's Ride* (Oxford University Press, 1994) and Jane Triber's concise pamphlet, "The Midnight Ride of Paul Revere: From History to Folklore" (Paul Revere House, undated). Esther Forbes's *Paul Revere and the World He Lived In* (Little, Brown, 1942) won the Pulitzer Prize. Michael M. Greenburg's *The Court-Martial of Paul Revere: A Son of Liberty and America's Forgotten Military Disaster* (University Press of New England, 2014) focuses on Revere's disastrous military career. Triber's *A True Republican: The Life of Paul Revere* (University of Massachusetts, 1998) explores how Revere's role as an artisan shaped his politics, and Alfred F. Young's *The Shoemaker and the Tea Party: Memory and the American Revolution* (Beacon Press, 2000) offers a more general look at how members of the working class and not just the wealthy shaped the Revolution.

Paul Revere's Three Accounts of His Famous Ride (Massachusetts Historical Society, 1968) reprints Revere's own versions. The first two were probably written in 1775 at the request of the Massachusetts Congress, and the third, undated, years later.

CHAPTER NINE: POOR RICHARD

Gordon Wood's *The Americanization of Benjamin Franklin* (Penguin Press, 2004) incisively chronicles how Franklin came to be seen as the symbol of America—in France while he lived and in America after he died. Walter Isaacson's *Benjamin Franklin: An American Life* (Simon & Schuster, 2003), a more comprehensive biography, reveals much about Franklin's own efforts to create a new American archetype.

Franklin's autobiography is available in many editions, including a convenient paperback from the Library of America (1990).

CHAPTER TEN: ELBOW ROOM

Meredith Mason Brown's *Frontiersman* (Louisiana State University Press, 2008), Robert Morgan's *Daniel Boone: Daniel Boone and the Making of America* (Algonquin Books, 2007), and Michael Lofaro's *Daniel Boone: An American Life* (University Press of Kentucky, 2003) are excellent biographies. John Mack Faragher's *Daniel Boone: The Life and Legend of an American Pioneer* (Henry Holt, 1992) is a fascinating look at both the life and the legend. J. Gray Sweeney's *The Columbus of the Wood: Daniel Boone and the Typology of Manifest Destiny* (Washington University Gallery of Art, 1992) studies Boone myths in nineteenth-century art. Richard Slotkin wrote a trilogy on frontier myths; the first volume, *Regeneration through Violence: The Mythology of the American Frontier, 1600–1860* (Wesleyan University Press, 1973), presents Boone as an archetypal American hero.

Lyman Draper's unfinished biography is available in print, edited by Ted Franklin Belue and titled *The Life of Daniel Boone* (Stackpole Books, 1998). Other primary sources, including John Filson's *The Discovery, Settlement and present State of Kentucke: And an Essay towards the Topography and Natural History of that important Country: To which is added, An Appendix, Containing . . . The Adventures of Col. Daniel Boon, one of the first*

Settlers and Timothy Flint's *The First White Man of the West or the Life and Exploits of Col. Daniel Boone* . . . are available online.

CHAPTER ELEVEN: THE INDIAN GUIDE

Donna J. Kessler's *The Making of Sacagawea: A Euro-American Legend* (University of Alabama Press, 1996) is the most comprehensive account of the various legends surrounding Sacagawea. Also useful are *Lewis & Clark and the Indian Country: The Native American Perspective*, edited by Frederick E. Hoxie and Jay T. Nelson (University of Illinois Press, 2007), *Exploring Lewis and Clark: Reflections on Men and Wilderness* by Thomas P. Slaughter (Knopf, 2003), *Lewis and Clark: Journey to Another America*, edited by Alan Taylor (Missouri Historical Society Press, 2003), *Twenty Thousand Roads: Women, Movement, and the West* by Virginia Scharff (University of California Press, 2003), and *Lewis & Clark Among the Indians* by James P. Ronda (University of Nebraska Press, 1998; originally published in 1984).

Popular histories of the expedition include Dayton Duncan's and Ken Burns's *Lewis & Clark: The Journey of the Corps of Discovery* (Knopf, 1997), Stephen E. Ambrose's *Undaunted Courage: Meriwether Lewis, Thomas Jefferson, and the Opening of the American West* (Simon & Schuster, 1996), and David Lavender's *The Way to the Western Sea: Lewis & Clark Across the Continent* (Harper & Row, 1988).

Grace Raymond Hebard makes her case for Sacagawea's long life in *Sacajawea: A Guide and Interpreter of the Lewis and Clark Expedition* (Dover Publications, 2002, originally published in 1932).

The Lewis and Clark Journals: An American Epic of Discovery, edited by Gary E. Moulton (University of Nebraska Press, 2003), is an abridged version of the definitive edition.

CHAPTER TWELVE: KING OF THE WILD FRONTIER

Valuable biographies include Michael Wallis's *David Crockett: The Lion of the West* (W.W. Norton, 2011), Mark Derr's *The Frontiersman: The Real Life and the Many Legends of Davy Crockett* (William Morrow, 1993), Richard Boyd Hauck's *Crockett: A Bio-Bibliography* (Greenwood, 1982), and James Atkins Shackford's *Davy Crockett: The Man and the Legend*

(University of North Carolina Press, 1956). Also valuable for a range of perspectives on the mythical Crocketts are two collections of essays edited by Michael A. Lofaro, *Davy Crockett: The Man, The Legacy, The Legend* (University of Tennessee Press, 1985) and *Crockett at Two Hundred: New Perspectives on the Man and the Myth*, co-edited by Joe Cummings (University of Tennessee Press, 1989).

Shackford and Stanley Folmsbee provided useful annotations to a facsimile edition of the one book in whose writing Crockett actually participated, *A Narrative of the Life of David Crockett* (University of Tennessee Press, 1973, originally published in 1834). The other books supposedly written by Crockett can be found online. Richard M. Dorson selected and edited Crockett stories from the almanacs in *Davy Crockett, American Comic Legend* (Spiral Press, 1939). Dorson's selections are somewhat sanitized, leaving out many that would have been as offensive to his readers in the first half of the twentieth century as they would be in the twenty-first. His book remains necessary, since many of the almanacs remain hard to find.

CHAPTER THIRTEEN: APPLE SEEDS
Recent studies include William Kerrigan's scholarly *Johnny Appleseed and the American Orchard: A Cultural History* (Johns Hopkins University Press, 2012) and Howard Means's lively *Johnny Appleseed: The Man, the Myth, the American Story* (Simon & Schuster, 2011). Michael Pollan offers his provocative interpretation of Appleseed in *The Botany of Desire: A Plant's-Eye View of the World* (Random House, 2001), and Robert Morgan puts Appleseed in the context of other frontier figures in *Lions of the West: Heroes and Villains of the Westward Expansion* (Algonquin Books, 2011). Robert Price's *Johnny Appleseed: Man and Myth* (Indiana University Press, 1954) was the first thorough study of both man and myth and remains valuable.

CHAPTER FOURTEEN: ABNER DOUBLEDAY'S GAME
John Thorn's *Baseball in the Garden of Eden: The Secret History of the Early Game* (Simon & Schuster, 2011) ranges well beyond Doubleday and Cartwright to tell the stories of others with stronger claims to having

invented baseball. David Block's *Baseball Before We Knew It: A Search for the Roots of the Game* (University of Nebraska Press, 2005) and Robert Henderson's *Ball, Bat, and Bishop: The Origin of Ball Games* (University of Illinois Press, 2001, originally published in 1947) both make the case for baseball's evolution rather than invention.

The origins of the Hall are covered in Jim Reisler's *A Great Day in Cooperstown: The Improbable Birth of Baseball's Hall of Fame* (Carroll & Graf, 2006) and James A. Vlasich's *A Legend for the Legendary: The Origin of the Baseball Hall of Fame* (Bowling Green State University Popular Press, 1990).

Albert G. Spalding's *America's National Game* (Lincoln: University of Nebraska Press, 1992, originally published in 1911) draws on not only Spalding's recollections but also the writings and scrapbooks of Henry Chadwick.

Chapter Fifteen: Ain't I a Woman?

Of modern biographies of Truth, Nell Irwin Painter's *Sojourner Truth: A Life, a Symbol* (Norton, 1996) and Carleton Mabee's *Sojourner Truth* (New York University Press, 1993) make the case she never said "Ain't I a woman," while Margaret Washington's *Sojourner Truth's America* (University of Illinois Press, 2009) and Erlene Stetson and Linda David's *Glorying in Tribulation: The Lifework of Sojourner Truth* (Michigan State University Press, 1994) argue that Truth might have said it. Mabee's 1998 article in the *New England Quarterly*, "Sojourner Truth and President Lincoln" is also useful.

The 1884 edition of *Narrative of Sojourner Truth* is available with an introduction and notes by Painter (Penguin, 1998).

Chapter Sixteen: The Log Cabin

Valuable books on the evolution of Lincoln's image include Jackie Hogan's *Lincoln, Inc.: Selling the Sixteenth President in Contemporary America* (Rowman & Littlefield, 2011), Barry Schwartz's *Abraham Lincoln in the Post-Heroic Era: History and Memory in Late Twentieth-Century America* (University of Chicago Press, 2008), Edward Steers Jr.'s *Lincoln Legends: Myths, Hoaxes, and Confabulations Associated with Our Greatest President*

(University Press of Kentucky, 2007), Schwartz's *Abraham Lincoln and the Forge of National Memory* (University of Chicago Press, 2000), Merrill D. Peterson's *Lincoln in American Memory* (Oxford University Press, 1994), Don E. Fehrenbacher's *Lincoln in Text and Context: Collected Essays* (Stanford University Press, 1987), Stephen B. Oates's *Abraham Lincoln: The Man Behind the Myths* (Harper & Row, 1984), Roy P. Basler's *The Lincoln Legend: A Study in Changing Conceptions* (Houghton Mifflin, 1935), and Lloyd Lewis's *Myths After Lincoln* (Harcourt, Brace, 1929). David Herbert Donald's *Lincoln Reconsidered: Essays on the Civil War Era* (Vintage Books edition, 2001) includes a number of essays stressing the importance of studying Lincoln myths as well as reality.

Of early biographies, *Herndon's Lincoln* by William H. Herndon and Jesse W. Weik is available in print, edited by Douglas L. Wilson and Rodney O. Davis (University of Illinois Press, 2006). Others are available online, including Gilbert Holland's *The Life of Abraham Lincoln*. Carl Sandburg's six volumes can be found in various editions, including a one-volume condensation.

By 1932, so many books had been written on Lincoln that James Thurber wrote a humorous essay imagining Congress passed a law outlawing new ones without a permit. The penalty for a new Lincoln biography was a maximum fine of $50,000 and up to two years in prison, or both, according to Thurber's contact at the "Bureau of Publishing Statistics and Biographers' Permits." Had Thurber's fictional bureau actually existed, it's unlikely it could have slowed the proliferation of new biographies, and even Thurber might have admitted some of them were well worth reading. Of the many important modern biographies, Donald's *Lincoln* (Simon & Schuster, 1995) and Oates's *With Malice Toward None: The Life of Abraham Lincoln* (Harper & Row, 1977) are balanced and very readable.

William Hanchett's *The Lincoln Murder Conspiracies* (University of Illinois Press, 1983) includes a thorough refutation of Eisenschiml's conspiracy theory, and Edward Steers Jr.'s *Blood on the Moon: The Assassination of Abraham Lincoln* (University Press of Kentucky, 2001) debunks all sorts of myths that surround the assassination.

CHAPTER SEVENTEEN: THE LOST CAUSE

David Blight's *Race and Reunion: The Civil War in American Memory* (Belknap Press, 2001) is forceful and persuasive about how white unity came at the expense of black rights. Other worthwhile books on how the Civil War has been remembered include Will Kaufman's *The Civil War in American Culture* (Edinburgh University Press, 2006), William C. Davis's *The Cause Lost: Myths and Realities of the Confederacy* (University Press of Kansas, 1996), Gaines M. Foster's *Ghosts of the Confederacy: Defeat, the Lost Cause, and the Emergence of the New South* (Oxford University Press, 1987), and Robert Penn Warren's *The Legacy of the Civil War* (Harvard University Press, 1983, originally published in 1961).

On the literature of the Civil War, Daniel Aaron's *The Unwritten War: American Writers and the Civil War* (Knopf, 1973) is comprehensive, and Edmund Wilson's *Patriotic Gore: Studies in the Literature of the American Civil War* (Oxford University Press, 1962), though overly sympathetic to Lost Causers, is nonetheless filled with insights on southern and northern writers. Thomas Nelson Page's and Joel Chandler Harris's books are available online.

Tony Horwitz's *Confederates in the Attic: Dispatches from the Unfinished Civil War* (Vintage, 1998) shows how the Lost Cause still resonates throughout the South in ways both tragic and funny.

CHAPTER EIGHTEEN: THE NOBLE OUTLAW

James P. Muehlberger's *The Lost Cause: The Trials of Frank and Jesse James* (Westholme, 2013) examines court proceedings involving the James brothers. T. J. Stiles's *Jesse James: Last Rebel of the Civil War* (Knopf, 2002) puts to rest any doubts about James (and his legend) arising out of the Civil War and Reconstruction, not the frontier. William A. Settle Jr.'s *Jesse James Was His Name* (University of Missouri Press, 1966) remains valuable for its systematic effort to distinguish facts from fictions.

Some scholarly debate has surrounded the idea that James was a "social bandit," a phrase E. J. Hobsbawm used in *Bandits* (New Press, 2000, originally published in 1969) to describe outlaws who were seen as heroes because they fought injustice. Among the important critiques of Hobsbawm's work is Richard White's "Outlaw Gangs of the Middle

Border" (*Western Historical Quarterly,* October 1981). Richard Slotkin also weighs in on this topic and on James myths in general in *Gunfighter Nation: The Myth of the Frontier in Twentieth-Century America* (Atheneum, 1992).

A collection edited by Harold Dellinger, *Jesse James: The Best Writings on the Notorious Outlaw and His Gang* (Globe Pequot, 2007), includes selections from the nineteenth, twentieth, and twenty-first centuries.

Chapter Nineteen: Steel-Driving Man

Scott Reynolds Nelson's *Steel Drivin' Man: The Untold Story of An American Legend* (Oxford University Press, 2006) is both a history of the mythical John Henry and a detective story about tracking down the real John Henry. Brett Williams's *John Henry: A Bio-Bibliography* (Greenwood Press, 1983) offers comprehensive coverage of John Henry in song, literature, and art. Louis W. Chappell's *John Henry: A Folk-Lore Study* (Kennikat Press, 1933) and Guy B. Johnson's *John Henry: Tracking Down a Negro Legend* (University of North Carolina Press, 1929) remain useful for their early and competing efforts to track both the ballad and the man.

Chapter Twenty: The Wild West

The best book on both the man and his show is Louis S. Warren's *Buffalo Bill's America: William Cody and the Wild West Show* (Knopf, 2005). Other useful books are Deanne Stillman's *Blood Brothers: The Story of the Strange Friendship between Sitting Bull and Buffalo Bill* (Simon & Schuster, 2017), Sandra K. Sagala's *Buffalo Bill on Stage* (University of New Mexico Press, 2008), Larry McMurtry's *The Colonel and Little Missie: Buffalo Bill, Annie Oakley, and the Beginnings of Superstardom in America* (Simon & Schuster, 2005), Robert A. Carter's *Buffalo Bill Cody: The Man Behind the Legend* (John Wiley & Sons, 2000), and Joy S. Kasson's *Buffalo Bill's Wild West: Celebrity, Memory, and Popular History* (Hill and Wang, 2000). *Gunfighter Nation: The Myth of the Frontier in Twentieth-Century America,* the third volume in Richard Slotkin's trilogy (Atheneum, 1992), includes an extensive analysis of the man and show.

The Frontier in American Life, a volume edited by James R. Grossman, was created to accompany an exhibition at the Newberry Library (University of California, 1994) and includes a valuable essay by Richard White, "Frederick Jackson Turner and Buffalo Bill." *Buffalo Bill and the Wild West*, a volume created to accompany an exhibition at the Brooklyn Museum, the Museum of Art, Carnegie Institute, and Buffalo Bill Historical Center (Brooklyn Museum, 1981), includes useful essays as well as illustrations.

Index